Keep to the Left!

Al

Best wishes

Jesse Lovelace

IRELAND

SEPTEMBER 2000

Keep to the Left!

Freewheeling through Ireland

Jesse N. Lovelace

WRITERS CLUB PRESS
San Jose New York Lincoln Shanghai

Keep to the Left!
Freewheeling through Ireland

Writers Club Press
an imprint of iUniverse, Inc.

For information address:
iUniverse, Inc.
5220 S. 16th St., Suite 200
Lincoln, NE 68512
www.iuniverse.com

ISBN: 0-595-23931-5

Printed in the United States of America

To the generations of my past—my maternal ancestors: the Welshes, the Larkins, the Darbys, and the McGraths, whose descendants sought a new life by sailing to this continent; to the Lovelaces who had a hand in building a new nation in Maryland, Virginia, Kentucky and Minnesota. To my parents, Robert Lovelace and Cecilia Welsh, who proved that Irish Catholic and English Protestant can be compatible. To my own generation, who have proved that Irish and Italian can also be compatible. To my daughters (and their husbands), who seem to have taken the best of both their parents. To my grandchildren, Katie, Andy, and Marcus, the little laughing, singing spirits who will speak of us when we are gone and give us immortality.

Go now, my good friend, to Doolin
And stand on the cliff tops so high.
Reach with both hands to the heavens,
And claim your share of the sky.

Journey, my good friend, to Cashel
And stand in the cathedral in awe.
Walk where Brian the High King
Once governed with justice and law.

Travel, my good friend, to Dingle
And watch the waves in the bay.
Savor the soft Gaelic singing
And peat smoke at the end of the day.

Return then, my good friend, from Ireland
With your heart uplifted and free.
Remember forever the castles
And green fields running down to the sea.

J.L.

Contents

PREFACE

I wish to emphasize that this is definitely not a travel guide. It is simply a narration of a tremendous experience in my life, which I wish to share with the reader. I make no claim to absolute historical or geographical accuracy; this is not a work of scholarship in any way.

One does not have to *be* Irish to enjoy the Irish. All things Celtic have become chic in recent years, sometimes to the point of excess, but the awful stereotypes are slowly fading, for which I'm grateful. The grotesque caricatures, such as the Notre Dame mascot, are on the way out. The foolishness of St. Patrick's Day celebrations—green beer, green foam rubber hats and ears, Worst Irish Tenor contests and the like—are gradually disappearing. New experiments in Irish music, art and literature are becoming part of the mainstream. My intention is to offer my impressions of the place where it all started.

In the portion of the text dealing with our time in Ireland, I have kept to British grammar and spelling as much as possible to conform with English spelling in Ireland—switching between American and British usage can be confusing, and I wished to avoid it.

I can't vouch for the correct spelling of names, especially of people we met along the way. If I have misspelled a name, I apologize and assure you that it was not intentional.

You will notice the occasional use of the notorious "F" word. I used it only in reporting what I had heard, or where I deemed it appropriate. I tried to soften its shock value by spelling it somewhat phonetically and as close as possible to Irish pronunciation, which varies considerably, depending on locale. In addition, in

Father Andrew Greeley's novel *Irish Gold*, his main character, Nuala McGrail, a charming, intelligent, passionate beautiful lass, uses it in every other sentence. If it's acceptable for a priest to use it in his writing, and for the lovely Nuala to use it so offhandedly, I figured it should be acceptable for me.

Another word that might puzzle the reader is "eejit." This is simply the Irish pronunciation of "idiot." I think the Irish word conveys a great deal more contempt and disgust than the usual spelling and pronunciation.

The reader might also perceive that we spent much time in Irish pubs and seemed to have consumed large quantities of Guinness. I don't want to leave the impression that we are excessive drinkers. Due to a complex tax system, the amount of alcohol in Irish beer is much less than in American beer, and to get inebriated would require a great capacity for liquid. One is more likely to feel full before getting drunk. Moreover, social drinking is an integral part of Irish culture, and pubs in Ireland are community centers where people gather to converse, relax, and discuss the latest topic of interest. We frequented pubs to soak up the atmosphere, get information, and meet people in a natural environment on their own terms and ours, rather than being herded around in a guided tour.

You will probably notice that I use the phrase "a powerful thirst," quite often. We picked that one up from Michaeleen Flynn, Barry Fitzgerald's irascible character in the movie *The Quiet Man*. Michaeleen is the archetypical Irish pub patron, so we used his favorite phrase whenever we were about to go into a pub. We enjoyed the outrageous exaggeration of the statement so much that it became a kind of catchword.

Quite frequently in the text and especially in reference to pubs, I have used the Gaelic word *craic* (pronounced "crack"). There's no single word for it in English. The word connotes good times, enjoyable company, good drinks, engaging conversation, and great music and song. The word pretty well describes our trip. As the Irish say, "Indeed, the *craic* was mighty!"

ACKNOWLEDGEMENTS

I would be remiss if I did not recognize the help so generously given in putting this all together—both our trip and the writing of this book. Thanks are due to my daughters and their husbands for putting up with our eccentricities and foibles: to Laurice and Steve Magill for all the little matters, such as transportation to the airport and caring for our dog; to Santina and Dan King for their constant encouragement to take the trip of a lifetime.

Many thanks are due to our good friends Carl and Kathy Melling for their constant encouragement and support, and their proofreading and helpful suggestions.

Above all, my thanks and love go to my wife, my friend, my most excellent traveling companion Micki. She has the unique ability to blend the practical and romantic, whereas I tend to wander off into irrelevancy. Without her natural skill in photography; her ability to observe, remember and take accurate notes; and her adaptability and good humor, this narrative would not have been possible.

GO RAIBH MAITH AGAT.

INTRODUCTION

Once upon a time, back in the middle thirties, in the midst of the Great Depression, two young people met and fell in love in the small Minnesota town of Eyota. She was a country school teacher, and he was a veterinarian's assistant. Times were hard for them economically, as they were for nearly every working class couple in those days, but they had a few additional things to contend with. She was the daughter of Irish Catholic immigrants, and he came from a Protestant family that had first come to America from England in the seventeenth century.

In spite of all difficulties, they married. The families on both sides were outraged and refused to speak with the young couple for over a year. Finally, the young man's sister, a staunch Methodist with no great love for Catholics of any stripe, much less bog Irish, nevertheless decided that enough was enough, and told the young couple that their beliefs were their own business, and no one had the right to cast them out.

The young woman's family decided that they would look pretty bad if they were outclassed in tolerance by a bunch of heathen Protestants, and so decided that maybe they should back off too. So it came about that nearly two years after their marriage, the young woman took her husband to meet his Irish in-laws. The young couple were my parents, Cecilia Welsh and Robert Lovelace.

My Dad always relished telling about meeting his Ulster-born mother-in-law for the first time. The Welshes lived in a big old ramshackle house in the tiny village of Amiret, Minnesota. The kitchen was a huge room in the back of the house where my

Grandma Liz spent most of her time in front of a giant wood range.

According to Dad's telling of it, he and my mother walked into the kitchen while Grandma was bent over checking loaves of bread in the oven. Grandma was not very tall, but was nearly as wide as she was high, and quite broad in the beam. Dad said that his first view of Liz was about an acre of calico.

There was a slight awkward pause as my mother tried to come up with the most appropriate greeting. She finally said simply, "Ma, this is Bob." Grandma Liz stood up, turned around, and with a dead serious expression on her face, walked over to a corner and picked up a broom. Without a word, she marched up to Dad, thrust the broom at him and stated, "Here. Hit me in the arse. I burned the bread." All was well.

With that delightful tale in the background, I could hardly avoid growing up with a sense of being Irish, but the state of Irish culture in America at the time was pretty sad. Music consisted mostly of sentimental tunes about returning to the Emerald Isle, a trip very few Irish-Americans ever actually took. The experiences of their parents and grandparents were apparently so horrible that it was best to wax nostalgic from a safe distance.

In the fifties, interest in Ireland began to grow, albeit slowly. When the classic *The Quiet Man* hit the screen, I went to see it but didn't get a whole lot out of it except a twelve year old's fascination with a mile long brawl, and a life long crush on Maureen O'Hara.

When I was in college, the great folk music craze was at its height. Most of the folk groups of the time were particularly awful, singing heartfelt but brainless work songs when it was obvious that most of the singers didn't know a shovel from a pickaxe. The extremely clean-cut Kingston Trio and the Limelighters singing songs about laying track and digging coal didn't quite ring true.

But one group grabbed my attention: the very proudly Irish Clancy Brothers and Tommy Makem. They stood out with the authenticity of their music and the extreme contrast with much of the sappy stuff that passed for Irish music in America at the time—"When Irish Eyes are Smiling," "McNamara's Band," the usual junk hauled out on St. Patrick's Day. The Clancys had a wit and the ability to slide from angry Irish rebel anthems to wild hilarious self-mockery to haunting ballads with an ease that suggested the finely tuned Irish sense of the power of poetry and music.

As an English major at St. John's University in Minnesota, I also had the very good fortune to have taken classes on William Butler Yeats and James Joyce from the incomparable Steve Humphrey, one of the most literate and cultured men I have ever known. It was years before I even came close to understanding what Yeats and Joyce were talking about, but I think Professor Humphrey knew that would happen and laid the groundwork for it.

As time went on, I occasionally hauled out the old Clancy LP's for a bit of nostalgia. The Irish Rovers made a brief appearance on the music scene and I bought most of their albums. The Rovers also had a weekly television variety show on Canadian TV, which we could get on our local public television channel. The show was a mix of music, dance and comedy, all with a distinct Irish flavor.

I think that my consciousness of Irishness was sharpened most by two events: the eruption in the early seventies of the current round of The Troubles in Northern Ireland and the publication of Leon Uris's novel *Trinity*. Uris put the modern conflict in historical perspective; his companion book *Ireland: A Terrible Beauty*, gorgeously photographed by his wife Jill, complemented his fiction with facts and visual images. With a more concrete perception of where my Irish ancestors came from, I became more active in learning about Irish culture.

As the years went by, and our daughters Laurice and Santina grew up, all of us became more involved in anything Celtic. The girls like to tell everyone that they knew the words to "One-Eyed Reilly" before they knew "Now I lay me down to sleep." We attended concerts by Irish musicians whenever we could—Phil Coulter, The Chieftains, even the Clancy Brothers and Tommy Makem. I was even lucky enough to meet and talk with Pat, Bobby, Liam, and Tommy on several occasions. I found them to be gracious and congenial gentlemen, willing to sign autographs and pose for pictures. Having a Jameson with Pat was a highpoint in my life.

When my daughter Laurice married Steve Magill in 1993, we managed to celebrate the wedding with strong Irish overtones—a piper at the church and Tommy Makem's "Red is the Rose" played at the wedding dance.

Santina married Dan King in 1996 and added more Celtic flavor to her wedding—an outside ceremony in a grove of trees, a piper, and a banner depicting the Claddagh symbol (a heart, hands and crown) and the Gaelic word *Fáilte* (Welcome). She also gave me the opportunity to give a short speech explaining the origins of the symbol: hands for friendship, a heart for love, and a crown for loyalty.

The Kings spent their honeymoon in Ireland and fell in love with the country and its people. They regaled us with stories of kindly treatment by everyone they had met and descriptions of the world's most inspiring scenery. At Christmas, Santina gave me a picture Dan had taken at the Cliffs of Moher—a lovely portrait of herself in an Aran sweater, with her long auburn hair floating in the sea wind. Opposite her picture is William Butler Yeats' poem "I am of Ireland." I still keep that picture displayed.

That pretty well clinched it—I could no longer act the role of Irish patriarch without ever having visited the place. And so we began to prepare our journey.

PREPARATIONS

After Santina and Dan's wedding in August 1996, the gradual tentative planning for our big trip began. Instead of saying "If we ever get to Ireland..." after an Irish concert or cultural event, we started saying "When we ever get to Ireland..."

Our preparations got a boost in January 1998 when Micki unexpectedly got the opportunity to travel to Europe. Edith Messerich, a long-time family friend, wanted to visit Europe and needed a traveling companion and chauffeur. Micki jumped at the chance, since the itinerary included a tour through Calabria in southern Italy, where a good number of her cousins still live. Her adventures through Germany, Austria, and Italy were sometimes hair-raising, but never dull. The events of her journey are far too complicated to relate here, but they did have one result: If Micki could visit the home of her ancestors, then it was only right that I should visit my ancestors' native country.

We had visited the Black Hills in South Dakota several times in the past decade, having been introduced to the place when Dan and Santina worked there during their college days. In 1994, we held a mini-family reunion in a cabin at Custer State Park. Dan and Santina were working in the park at the time and arranged a few things for us. Laurice and Steve, my brother Bill and his wife Sue, Dan and Santina, and the two of us plus the family dog Anika spent a week of fishing, exploring, outrageous conversation, and hefty consumption of amber fluids.

What does a trip to the Black Hills have to do with a journey to Ireland? We enjoyed our time in Custer State Park so much that we spent several subsequent vacations there, always in September when the weather was cool and the crowds of tourists were gone.

In September 1999, while sitting in front of our cabin on a crisp clear evening, we reached the decision. We'd spent a satisfying day trout fishing, and we were now relaxing in front of a campfire enjoying a sip of Jack Daniels. In a state of relaxed euphoria, we made the final decision: next year at this time, we'll be in Ireland.

We made our intentions well known to everyone, probably with the notion that if we talked about it often enough, we couldn't back down. Our good friends the Mellings gave me as a Christmas present Frommer's *Ireland from $50 a Day.* This proved to be a valuable resource; if the book couldn't tell you, it told you where to find out. We discussed the information so often that we began referring to the book as a person—"Frommer says…"

We contacted the Irish Tourist Board and asked them to send us materials. They responded swiftly with a huge packet of information that was an immense help in getting our ideas together.

By March we arranged vacation time with our employers. We worked out a tentative itinerary and then altered it a half dozen times. By mid April, we had figured out a plan that was fairly definite, but open to change if the need arose. We called several travel agencies about making arrangements but found most packages to be unsatisfactory—either too restrictive, too short or too expensive.

We finally called Aer Lingus (the Irish airline) directly and booked tickets for a flight on Sunday September 3, 2000 with a return flight on Sunday September 24. Aer Lingus doesn't fly into Minneapolis, the nearest international airport, but does have connections into Chicago O'Hare. They also have a cooperative agreement with American Airlines, and so arranged a flight on American to Chicago and a transfer to Aer Lingus and a direct flight from there to Shannon International in Ireland. Aer Lingus also reserved a rental car for us, which would be picked up right at the airport on arrival.

"Frommer said" that it is a good idea to book lodgings in advance for the first and last nights' stay in Ireland, and also any nights we'd be staying in Dublin, as getting accommodations in the city on the spot can be chancy. We had picked September as a time to go because we figured the summer tourist crowds would not be as thick. On the other hand, sports tournaments are scheduled in Dublin in September, and lodging can be tight.

In April I called Maeve Fitzgerald at Churchfield B&B in Doolin on the coast of County Clare and booked us for the nights of September 4 and 5. I told her we would be arriving early in the morning and would be in Doolin sometime before noon. Maeve said our room would be ready and that we should call her from the airport so she could anticipate our arrival. She said that we would be very tired and would need a nap when we got there. She told us that we were definitely going to rest for a few hours, and that the room would be waiting for us. She sounded like a lady that brooks no argument. I asked her if she needed a deposit, but she said it wasn't necessary. Later she did send us a lovely post card with a delicate ink sketch of the Doolin coast. The postcard confirmed our reservation.

I then phoned Peggie Massey and reserved three nights at her B&B in the Dublin suburb of Ballsbridge for the nights of September 11, 12, and 13. I picked Peggie's out of the Town & Country Homes Association book that the Tourist Board had sent us. It turned out to be an excellent choice. Peggie required a reservation of at least half the price, so I sent her a check in US currency for what I guessed would be the entire amount. If there was any difference, we could settle up when we got there.

We made our last advanced booking (again on Frommer's recommendation) at Ardmayle House outside Cashel in County Tipperary for the nights of September 18 and 19. I wanted to try my hand at fly-fishing in the River Suir, which abuts the property. I didn't talk to Annette Hunt, the owner of Ardmayle House, but the lady I talked to just took my name and said we were all taken care of. I asked her too if a deposit were required. She seemed taken a bit aback by the question and replied

"Well, it's not really necessary, but if you want to, would twenty dollars be OK?" I sent her a check for the full amount.

The Tourist Board had assured us that in September, we'd have no problem booking reservations on a daily basis. We took their word for it, and decided that we could stay flexible. By the middle of May, we had all the necessities in place—airline tickets, a rental car, and enough accommodations.

For me there was one thing left. Over the years, I had tried with not much success to learn the basics of Gaelic, the Irish native language. My grandmother reputedly spoke it, but none of her children knew it, apart from a few dirty words. I had tried to learn a few rudimentary phrases from books, but whenever I tried them out on someone who spoke the language, all I'd get in reply was a puzzled stare. I finally stumbled onto a set of tapes that pretty much ignored the printed word and concentrated on memorizing spoken phrases. This system worked out pretty well. On my hour and a half round trip commute to work, I could play those tapes repeatedly. So all summer long, I listened to simple conversational Gaelic phrases every day until I thought I had most of them down. The big test would come when we got to Ireland.

We spent most of the summer impatiently counting down the days until we would be off. The time passed slowly, but it did pass. Labor Day weekend finally arrived. We had provided ourselves with enough cash in travelers' checks, both in American and English currency, and we were now completely ready.

On Saturday September 2, we loaded up the Chevy Blazer with all our luggage. We somehow wedged Anika, our goofy but amiable Siberian Husky, in between the suitcases and headed for Minneapolis. Laurice and Steve had generously offered to baby-sit the dog while we were gone. We spent that afternoon with the Magills, probably annoying them no end with our impatient nervousness.

A little after noon on Sunday, we bid our farewells to our grandkids Katie and Andy, to Anika, and to the ever-patient Steve, who stoically puts up with our antics. Laurice took us to Minneapolis-St. Paul International, dumped us off on the curb, wished us luck and left. We were now truly on our own.

We had no trouble or delay checking our bags and getting our boarding passes. We found our gate easily and waited for departure. At the proper time we were herded aboard and left the ground at 3:45.

Chicago is only a 50-minute flight from Minneapolis, so we were at O'Hare in very short order. This is where the panic of inexperienced travelers started to set in. We had landed at the domestic terminal, but had no idea how to reach the international terminal, where we were to connect with Aer Lingus. Fortunately for us, information stations were plentiful, and with a few directions, we navigated the maze of escalators and concourses until we found the rail shuttle to get us to our gate. Once in the correct terminal, we found our gate in short order.

Before we boarded, I looked out the window to get a look at our home for the night. There it was: the big green and white aircraft with a shamrock on the tail. There wasn't any doubt where that plane was heading.

Boarding was quick and orderly. We got our seats and settled in for the night. The next solid ground would be Ireland.

And the adventure began.

THE ROCKY ROAD TO DOOLIN

SEPTEMBER 4. We left O'Hare at 6:30 PM and were scheduled to arrive in Shannon at 7:30 AM local time. It was a very smooth and almost enjoyable flight: cute little Irish flight attendants and all the free Jameson Irish whiskey you could handle. The aircraft we settled into was an Airbus 330, the large size version. We had aisle seats in the centre section so getting up and moving around occasionally was fairly convenient. I can't sleep on an airplane as some fortunate folks can, and there's not much to see on a seven hour overnight flight, so I spent most of the time working on logic puzzles in a magazine I'd brought along. Sometime in the middle of the night, an attractive petite red haired flight attendant looked over my shoulder, poked me and exclaimed in mock disgust, "What is that?" I suppose flight attendants get bored on long trips too. At any rate, I appreciated the good-natured jibe.

Dawn was just breaking as we started the long descent into Shannon. Since there is no heavily populated area west of the airport, the land beneath us looked desolate and deserted, bog land mostly, interspersed with small ponds. Dark tones of brown and green were speckled with grey pools of open water, the whole scene highlighted with the reddish glint of the rising sun.

We landed at Shannon an hour ahead of schedule at 6:30AM due, I guess, to favourable winds. The airport is located way out in the middle of a bog and was completely deserted except for our plane. Our introduction to the Irish way of doing things started immediately. The ground crew couldn't get the jetway out from the building to reach the door of the plane. The captain apologized and said that they'd called an engineer at his home, but he was away and nobody knew where he was. The only thing for it was to pull up a rickety metal stairs to the door of the plane and we'd simply have to walk across the apron into the terminal, and "by the way, *Tá fáilte romhaibh go hÉireann*." (Welcome to Ireland)

So all the passengers got their carryon luggage from the overhead bins and filed out of the plane. This might have been an occasion for some irritation, but nobody seemed upset. The flight crew was so pleasant as we stepped out the door that the inconvenience seemed negligible. As we carefully stepped down the shaky stairway into the grey Irish dawn and walked the twenty yards to the terminal with our baggage in hand, I got a fleeting creepy feeling of what it must have been like for our ancestors to arrive in a new land.

The flight attendants were supposed to have handed out immigration forms to all the passengers to fill out before we landed, but evidently they ran out or missed some of us. We lined up at the immigration window and when our turn came, we were asked for the filled-out form. We didn't have one, so we were given one and asked to step out of the line and fill it out.

Filling out the form took only a few minutes, and when we got back into line, we moved toward the gate fairly quickly. There were four immigration stations, each with an officer taking the forms and stamping passports. When my turn came, the official stamped my passport, smiled and said, "Welcome to Ireland, Jesse." It was a small matter, but it made me feel pretty good. We had officially arrived.

After we went through immigration, we picked up the rest of our luggage, and headed for the customs area. The officials on duty were enjoying their morning coffee and didn't seem too interested in searching luggage. I guess we didn't look like sinister drug smugglers, so they passed us through with just a smile and a wave.

We checked in at the Avis desk, completed the paperwork for our rental car, and wheeled our overloaded baggage cart outside to the curb.

(Excuse me. It was a kerb. We're in Ireland now.) In a few minutes, a courtesy van pulled up; the driver loaded our luggage, told us to hop in, and shuttled us over to the Avis lot to pick up our car. I had reserved the cheapest rental available, so I expected some little English version of a Geo Metro, but instead we got a Renault Clio, a classy sort of compact halfway between a sedan and a station wagon.

After loading up the trunk (boot) and rear seat, we got into the front seat to get oriented. I wanted to be as familiar with the car's controls as possible before we set out. Sitting behind the wheel on the right side was a little disorienting at first, but we soon got familiar with the "backward" arrangement. I located all the switches and buttons and felt as ready as I was going to be.

We didn't take long to get comfortable. Clio (familiar name from now on) was a lot roomier on the inside than expected. It was even equipped with an "Oh, shit!" bar. This is what we have dubbed the little handle above the window on the passenger's side. Its purpose is to afford the rider a handgrip when in terrifying situations, while simultaneously yelling "OH, SHIT!"

We asked the Avis attendant for directions to Doolin, and he assured us that if we followed the road right next to us for a half-mile to the first roundabout, and then took the first left off that, we couldn't miss it. Full of ignorance, adrenalin, jet lag, and just plain terror, we started out. Chanting "Keep to the left! Keep to the left!," we approached the first roundabout.

I suppose we'd call a roundabout a traffic circle, but by any name, it's a very efficient way of handling traffic at intersections, especially when several roads come together as they usually do in Ireland. It consists of a circle in which traffic keeps going around clockwise. When a driver approaches the circle, he waits at a Yield sign until there is a clear opening in the circle, merges into it and follows the circle until he comes to the road he wants to follow. He then simply exits the circle and goes on his way. There is no stopping and waiting for a light, Drivers just enter and exit the circle in a continuous, if slow, motion. It's a lot smoother than traffic lights.

It was a good thing that it was early in the morning and traffic was light. Our map was little help. It didn't say anything about Irish roads being frighteningly narrow.

Our destination, Doolin (or Roadford, as some maps designate it), is about 35 miles from the airport and, ignorant as we were, we thought it would be a leisurely drive of less than an hour. At that first roundabout, which we negotiated quite skilfully, we turned onto N18 and headed toward Ennis. Actually, we didn't know about road numbers yet, and our maps left a lot out. At Ennis we turned onto N85 and then went through Fountain Cross and Inagh.

So far, so good. We kept on N85 to Ennistymon and then turned right onto N67, heading north to Lisdoonvarna. (If you'd like some information about this town in the summer, get a copy of Christy Moore's recording of "Lisdoonvarna." It's hilarious.) A mile or so short of "Lisdoon," as the locals call it, we turned onto R478, a regional road, and things got hairy.

The famous dry stone walls start right at the edge of the blacktop, the roads are very crooked and narrow, and we didn't have the foggiest idea where we were. I rounded a curve, going too fast, and hit a basketball-sized rock that had fallen onto the road. (The Oh, Shit! bar came into use here.) With great thumping noises coming from Clio's front end, I pulled into a driveway with that sinking feeling in the gut that I had torn the oil pan off. I checked under the car and found that the front wheel was bent into an ellipse and the wheel cover had disappeared, but there was no other damage. I found the jack and the spare in the boot and managed to change the wheel. We started on our way, rounded the next curve, slowly this time, and there was Doolin and the Atlantic, right where they were supposed to be.

Doolin is a tiny hamlet set on what looks like a 45-degree slope. We found Churchfield B&B immediately and rang the bell. It was only 10:30AM, but I'd had enough adventure to last quite a while.

I don't know what Maeve Fitzgerald, the lady of the house, thought when she answered the door. I was bedraggled and covered with dirt from changing the wheel, and I hadn't called her from the airport, as I had promised (no Irish money). We must have been quite a sight.

However, Maeve is a no-nonsense lady and a real gem. We explained what happened, and she briskly led us to our room, gave us advice on getting the wheel fixed, and more or less ordered us to take a nap. We gratefully complied.

When we were refreshed and calmed down, we were ready to do some exploring. Maeve runs a small grocery store/post office/change bureau on the ground floor of the house, so we changed some travellers' checks into Irish currency and set out.

We first went back up the hill to a petrol station Maeve had recommended to see about getting the wheel fixed. The guy there took one look at the mashed rim and said there was no way he could fix it. We'd have to find a larger place with more equipment and parts. Well, the spare was holding up, so we'd just have to keep looking.

We then went down to the ferry port to book passage to the Aran Islands, which aren't too far offshore from Doolin. The "port" is little more than a shabby concrete pier with a trailer house nearby for an office We checked on sailing times for the next day, then wandered around the shore for a while, took some pictures, and returned to the village.

Our first pub stop was Gus O'Connor's (established 1832, which in Ireland makes it a relatively new place). Actually, I did have an Irish £20 note with me when we left, but it was dedicated. In 1996, after Dan and Santina had returned from their honeymoon, Dan had given me the £20 note with strict instructions that it was to be spent on our first pint in Ireland, when we ever got there. I kept that bill for four years. We were now sitting in Gus O'Connor's Pub, Doolin, County Clare, and I was about to keep my word.

After sitting for about ten minutes waiting for table service, we watched the locals for the correct ordering procedure. You must go to the bar, place your order, pay for it and then wait for the Guinness to be drawn, and finally take it with you or go sit down and let the barman "drop it down to you." When we finally got our big black creamy topped pints, we found that indeed it *is* true: Guinness is only really good in Ireland.

As I took a long, slow sip of that fine brown brew, it hit me that in my wildest dreams, I never imagined that I would ever be casually sitting in a pub on the bleak but beautiful west coast of Ireland, but here we were. Imagination can turn into reality. We toasted to our good fortune and a satisfying adventure.

As it was now getting close to suppertime, we drove back to Churchfield, parked the car in the lot, and walked the fifty yards to McDermott's. We had read about this place in Frommer's and it came highly recommended for traditional music and good food. As we walked in the door, two guys, one with a guitar and the other with an accordion, were playing a selection of very old jigs and reels.

We took a seat across from the bar, in very plain view of the sign that states McDermott's philosophy: "If I had wanted to listen to an asshole, I would have farted." That pretty well summed up the ambience in here: everyone is welcome, but phonies enter at their own peril.

We ordered our pints and studied the menu for awhile. Three Americans soon joined us: a couple from Florida and an apparently single gal who had accompanied them on the plane over. We chatted a bit and then ordered our dinners. Before our meals were ready, we decided to move to a different table in order to be closer to the music. This was all right with the Florida couple, as they were going to leave as soon as they had eaten. The single lady joined us at our new table. She didn't order any dinner, but sat with us as we ate ours.

Micki ordered a roast lamb dinner, and I had a smoked salmon plate with brown bread. Our newfound friend seemed to think she was in some sort of theme park where the locals were hired to entertain tourists with their quaint behaviour. She kept getting up and talking to the musicians, making gushy fatuous remarks about how she loved Ireland.

About the time our dinners arrived, the musicians changed. The afternoon crew quit and was replaced by another bunch, also very good. Our American friend, who hadn't ordered dinner, kept helping herself to my basket of brown bread. Apparently she thought it was some sort of complimentary appetizer. To our relief, she soon bid us goodbye and left.

As the evening wore on, and the pints took their inevitable mellowing effect, the music got better and the crowd got friendlier. People bantered with each other, whether they knew each other or not. We of course knew absolutely nobody, but that didn't seem to make any difference. The local folks seemed to accept us and tacitly invited us to enjoy ourselves.

About the middle of the evening, 9:00 or so, the local patrons started putting up decorations: ribbons, streamers, balloons, etc. It seems that a local couple, two well-known musicians, was going to return that evening from their honeymoon, and McDermott's was putting on an impromptu celebration; anybody present was perfectly welcome to join the festivities.

The happy couple soon arrived to much cheering and clapping. The rest of the evening was spent in lively Irish music and dancing. So our day ended on a pretty happy note. We'd spent the evening drinking Guinness, enjoying the wonderful Irish hospitality, and getting acquainted with the country. Not a bad start.

THE OCEAN AND THE ISLANDS

SEPTEMBER 5. This is the day we sail to the Arans. We had a very restful night and started the day with a Full Irish Breakfast. (Caps deliberate.) We had heard of this legendary feast but didn't quite realize how huge it is.

B&B's take a great deal of pride in both their breakfasts and their dining rooms. This isn't a quick bowl of dry cereal on a Formica table—there is full silver, linen and china. The breakfast, sometimes known as an Ulster fry, almost invariably consists of breakfast sausage, black pudding (blood sausage), white pudding (liver sausage), bacon (more like Canadian bacon than American), toast and eggs, along with brown bread, hot cereal, and tea. This isn't just a list of choices; with the exception of the hot cereal, all this is on your plate.

After breakfast, we went down to the ferry port, got our tickets and waited until the ferry was ready to board. We overheard the captain warning a few passengers that if they chose to remain overnight on the islands, there would be no guarantee that the ferry would be back to pick them up tomorrow, since there was a storm predicted for the next day. When sailing time approached, we boarded the ferry (actually an old converted tugboat named "The Happy Hooker"), and sailed away to the Arans. There are three Aran Islands: Inisheer (East Island), Inishmaan (Middle Island), and Inishmore (Big Island). With a brief stop at Inishmaan to drop off a few passengers, we arrived in Kilronan, Inishmore, at 11AM.

We had intended to follow Frommer's recommendation and rent bikes for our tour of the island so we could careen around the country lanes like John Wayne and Maureen O'Hara, but one look at the hills convinced us to try another method. We are just too damned old for biking. The alternatives were a ride in a horse-drawn jaunting cart or a tour in a mini-bus. There were quite a few of both types available. Jaunting carts are two wheeled horse drawn vehicles with bench seats installed on each side facing outward over the wheels. The street from the harbour to the town was lined with carts and drivers waiting for passengers. Closer to town, minivans were parked along the street, likewise waiting for passengers. We thought the jaunting cart was just a bit touristy, so we opted for a min-bus tour.

We had decided to visit the Arans for several reasons. Micki, being a talented knitter, wanted to pick up some authentic patterns and native yarn for some sweater projects. I wanted to visit the *Gaeltacht*, the Gaelic-speaking areas of Ireland. The Arans are noted for their yarn, their distinctive sweater patterns and the fact that the natives all speak Gaelic among themselves. I had learned a few phrases of the language and I wanted to try it out. The cart and minivan drivers along the street all wore wool sweaters and were conversing in soft but rapid Gaelic. We'd certainly come to the right place.

A tall angular fellow with a rather beat up Toyota van caught our eye, so we hooked up with him. His name was Tom (99% of all Irishmen are named Tom, Kevin, or Eamon) and he looked like the stereotype of an islander: green eyes, tousled grey hair and a well-worn heather-hued Aran sweater.

We climbed aboard Tom's van, got settled in the middle set of seats and waited. There were two Asian ladies sitting on the bench in the back. They spoke fairly good English and greeted us pleasantly. Tom stuck his head in and said we'd get started as soon as he could get somebody to sit in the front seat. The two Asian ladies said something to each other and then got out and climbed into the front seat. Tom had meant that he was waiting for two more passengers to fill up the van, but the Asian ladies misunderstood him. Tom looked a little startled, but rather than embarrass them, he got behind the wheel and took off without a full load.

Tom gave us a pretty extensive tour of the island. We first visited a medieval cemetery known as the Seven Churches, a very early monastic site dating from around the eighth century. There are a number of chapels and buildings scattered around the place, interspersed with graves dating from before the Middle Ages right up to the 1990's. The cemetery is still used by the islanders. I was struck by the number of Mullins buried there. It must be the commonest name on the island.

Tom next took us down the road from the Seven Churches to a cluster of thatched houses. We all got out of the van to take some pictures, and while Micki and the Asian ladies were snapping away, Tom and I got to discussing roofs. "Guy stuff," building materials and tools, seems to be a pretty universal topic among males of all nationalities. He asked about shingles in our part of the US and then informed me that most new roofs in Ireland were now made of steel or slate. Thatched roofs are gradually becoming a thing of the past, although there are a good number of them still around, mainly in tourist areas. He seemed to think it was a shame that thatch was disappearing from the Irish landscape.

Our next stop was Dun Aengus, a Bronze Age Celtic fort, built around 500BC on a cliff on the western side of the island. Tom dropped us off at the visitor centre and said he'd be back in two hours to take us back to the ferry at Kilronan. It's about a half-mile walk from the visitor centre to the fort itself. As we started out on the path, we could hear music but couldn't tell where it was coming from. It felt a little eerie but not at all out of place. After all, the whole island is quite mysterious. The natives speak a language as old as the Stone Age, we were surrounded by ancient ruins, and the whole place just breathes antiquity. We rounded a corner and there was a guy sitting on a stool playing a concertina. With all the old rock walls and the little fields around us, the music just seemed to fit.

Dun Aengus is pretty impressive. It's built in three irregular semicircles of dry stone slate, stacked about 20 feet high. When it was built, the fort was circular, but portions of the cliff it sits on have fallen into the ocean, leaving the existing half circles of walls. Between the second and third rings is a field of sharp stone shafts slanted outward. The idea apparently was to foil any attack by horsemen or chariots. I guess that they had it figured out a long time ago what stones could do to wheels.

How an immense structure 2500 years old could survive this long without any mortar in the walls appears at first glance to be a little puzzling, but when you look at the stones, it's apparent that they are quite uniform in size and shape. Slate cracks and splits in fairly predictable patterns and the stones can be fitted quite tightly together to construct a very sturdy structure.

After a leisurely lunch at a picnic table at the visitor centre, Tom picked us up at the proper time and took us back to Kilronan. I thought that this would be a good time to try out my very basic Gaelic. On the coast of West Clare, Galway, and especially the Aran Islands, Gaelic is the first and exclusive language among the local people. (Later in the day we visited a pub where we were the only ones using English. It's a little disconcerting to see somebody yakking away in Gaelic on a cell phone.) When we got out of the van, I thanked Tom in Gaelic and asked him how much the tour was. It was only £5 apiece. He was courteous enough to act pleased and replied in simple enough words that I could understand him. That was kind of a thrill. He also informed me that people use the terms "Irish" and "Gaelic" interchangeably.

Micki shopped for Aran yarn and we visited a couple of pubs before the ferry left. The day was starting to cloud up and the wind was increasing. Since we were the last people on the ferry, all the seats inside were taken and we had to sit on a hatch cover out in the open. When we got out of Kilronan Harbour, the waves started slopping over the deck and we got drenched in a matter of minutes. An English lady sitting next to us offered us some of her space, remarking that she had waterproof pants. By that time, it was too late; we were already soaked to the skin.

I wasn't certain, but we didn't seem to be heading back on the same route we had taken that morning. Pretty soon the boat started slowing down and inching toward the shore of Inishmaan, the middle island. Around a little headland, there was a fishing boat, apparently without power, anchored dangerously close to some rocks. Evidently, the fishermen had radioed the ferry and we were now about to rescue them. A crewman tossed the fishing boat a line, they secured it, and we towed them to Inisheer. I felt like breaking into a chorus of "Home from the Sea," but I suppressed the urge. After we had dropped them off, the Happy Hooker took us back to Doolin without incident.

After we changed into some dry clothes at Maeve's, we walked down to McGann's Pub for supper. It was fairly crowded, but comfortable enough. We found out later in the trip that if you want a good seat close to the musicians, you have to arrive early in the evening. Our table was satisfactory and the crowd, a mix of locals and tourists, was pretty mellow.

The usual complement of animals was ambling around. Dogs and cats come in and out of pubs without any hindrance, and nobody seems to mind. A cat came wandering by our table and got a gentle shove from a waitress—"Out witcha! Go do somethin' useful!"

The dinner was delicious. Micki had a spiced chicken dish and I had baked salmon. Pub food, we were discovering to our delight, is delicious, plentiful and cheap.

Two incidents stand out about that night. The first was the Irish coffee episode. Everyone in the place was finishing up their dinners, and the word was going around that the Irish coffee was terrific. People were going up to the bar and ordering for their table. The young fellow behind the bar was feeling the pressure, since he was whipping the cream by hand. (Nothing out of a pressurized can for these people). By the time I placed my order, he was getting pretty frazzled. When I told him I wanted two, he actually <u>did</u> it: something I always thought was a stage Irish caricature—he rolled his eyes heavenwards, let out a huge exaggerated sigh, and said, "Jaysus, Mary, and Joseph!" Later, I went back for a couple more, and when I got them, I left him £2 "for the Holy Family." He liked that one, laughed and gave me a thumbs up, and "Good one, mate!"

The second incident occurred on a trip to the bar. As I was making my way carefully through the crowd, I inadvertently bumped into a burly fellow about my age who was in deep conversation with a friend. I apologized, but he took no offence, and we got into a conversation. He asked "Y'from the States, then?" As if a twangy accent and an Eddie Bauer jacket weren't clues. I told him that yes, I was from Minnesota and introduced myself. This was the last real word I managed. He took it from there and never took a breath for 15 minutes. His name was Sean, he knew Minnesota well, and was impressed with how green it was. He knew all about Minnesota since he had flown over it once on a flight from Boston to Vancouver. The rest of the monologue was a sort of stream of consciousness recital of the wonders of the United States. Condensed version: "Y'live in a fine country, sir. The size of it! And the marvels of engineerin'! Take the Hoover Dam. What a piece of work it is! And speakin' of the Hoover Dam, the Empire State Buildin'! Built by the Mohawk Indians. Bravest people on earth, they are, to climb about a hundred stories up without a rope! Many of them died in the buildin' of it, y'know. Brave indeed! Well now, I'm playin' tonight and I must take me place. I enjoyed our conversation, and since ye're American, we'll play 'Turkey in the Straw' in yer honour." I didn't get to talk to him again, but when we left an hour later, a definitely West Clare version of "Turkey in the Straw" followed us out the door.

We walked up the road to McDermott's for a little more music and a nightcap of a couple of Paddys before we crossed the street and turned in. So our second day in Ireland included an ancient Celtic fort, listening to Gaelic, getting soaked on the Atlantic, several pints, Irish coffee, Irish whiskey, Irish music, and Irish bullshit. I think we pretty well covered the basics.

TAKE ME HOME TO MAYO

SEPTEMBER 6. We arose at 7AM and went down to another of Maeve's delicious huge breakfasts. One of the other guests at breakfast remarked that she had been down to McGann's last night to listen to traditional Irish music. The musicians were playing "Turkey in the Straw" as she walked in. "What in the world was that all about?"

We were hitting the road today and heading for County Mayo. After breakfast, Maeve dried the clothes we were wearing the day before, got out the fly rods I'd sent previously and booked us a B&B in Ballina, County Mayo. She immediately corrected my pronunciation without any apology: the name is <u>not</u> pronounced Bal-LEEN-a, but Bally-NAH.

We had brought our Town and Country Homes Association book along and had picked out a place in Ballina: Belvedere Bed & Breakfast. Maeve called the place for us and booked us a reservation for the evening. This is just another nice little courtesy in the system. One B&B will book the next one for you. Prices are very reasonable, only about $40 for two including that breakfast that sticks with you all day. With a system like that, food and lodging costs can be kept in line.

The Cliffs of Moher are only about 3 miles south of Doolin, so we took the slight detour to see them. The sun was out, but the wind off the ocean was very strong. The tour buses were pulling into the parking lot as we got there and unloading their contents. The wardens on each bus herded their charges into compact groups and shuffled them up the path to the scenic lookouts. Some of those poor old ladies were in dresses with heels and nylons, not quite the outfit to be climbing rocks in, especially in a gusty Atlantic wind. Watching some of the old guys tottering around wheezing and red-faced, I was afraid a few of them were going to cash in on the spot.

Once we reached the cliff edge, the view was spectacular. The Arans were visible and the long stretch of the cliffs either direction was incredible. The cliffs are said to average 700 feet from the ocean to the top. The drop is sheer and the breakers at the base are enormous, even though from that height, the expanse of the ocean looks quite calm. We took a few pictures, staggered back through the gale to the visitor centre for a cup of coffee and some respite from the wind. On the lee side of the building, it was warm and quite comfortable. We sat for a while at a picnic table watching the tour buses arrive and congratulating ourselves on being such adventurous and independent old farts.

We left the Cliffs just before noon and headed back through Doolin and up the coast road toward Galway. We took R479 and R477 through Fanore, Murroogh and Ballyvaughn, all along the shores of Galway Bay. The scenery was pretty spectacular, but I only saw it when we stopped for pictures. The road was extremely narrow and I didn't want a repeat of Monday's wheel episode.

We stopped at 12:30 at Ballyvaughn for a stretch and some pictures of the harbour. Right across from the parking lot was Monk's Pub. I recognized it from its appearance in nearly every coffee table book about Ireland. One thing I didn't recognize right away was the aroma of peat smoke in the air. It's quite a distinctive scent, something like burning leaves. From this point on, I don't think we ever got away from it entirely, even in Dublin. We had just a half pint at Monk's; we learned that a full pint (20 oz) can be a lot of liquid sloshing around in you, and rest stops are next to nonexistent in Ireland.

We had read in *Frommer's Guide* that the greatest seafood in Ireland was to be had at Moran's on the Weir, on the River Dunkellin just outside of Kilgolgan, County Galway. We had planned our route so we could stop there for lunch, which we did and were not disappointed. Moran's is a fairly upscale but old establishment where the seafood is taken out of the river (actually the mouth of the river) right outside the front door. Legend has it that Willie Moran caught 105 salmon in one morning in 1961 from the front step. (In Ireland, 1961 is something like this morning.)

Lunch consisted of a dozen grilled oysters and a plate of "dressed" prawns, a cold plate of shrimp with a mayonnaise dressing. It was delicious. We kept looking around for celebrities who are supposed to hang around there but we didn't see anybody we recognized.

After lunch we headed out again. Now we were on N18, a national road, and the progress was much faster. We negotiated 4 roundabouts on the outskirts of Galway City, got briefly off on the wrong road, but found the right track and headed up toward County Mayo. The Irish don't give directions by road numbers, but by the customary names of the roads. Unfortunately for foreigners, these names are not posted. We had been told to take the Headford Road; we had no idea where that was. We figured out that we were on the right path only when we passed through Headford.

The trip to Ballina was uneventful. We took N84 through Ballinrobe and Partry to Castlebar, and then N5, N58, and N26 to Ballina. With a population of 9000, Ballina is the largest town in Mayo. Belvedere, our B&B, was right on the highway on the edge of town. Our hosts, Tom and Mary Reily, were as gracious as Maeve Fitzgerald had been. The house is relatively new but built in a Neo-Georgian style that lends itself well to antique furnishings.

After a short rest, we headed downtown. It was only a 10-minute stroll to the heart of the town, so we left Clio behind. We intended to do some serious pub-crawling and I didn't feel up to driving on the left at night on narrow streets with a gut full of Guinness.

As a good-sized town by Irish standards, Ballina is an excellent place to get into the fine art of pubs. The plan was to snack and drink in as many establishments as time and commonsense would comfortably allow. We started our evening with a pint and a snack of pâté and chicken satay at the Bantra House Hotel lounge. Not exactly a typical pub, but much like every hotel bar in the world.

We visited about six pubs that night—I won't go into detail on every one, but they were all enjoyable. The level of conviviality depends on what sporting event happens to be on TV. Gaelic football and hurling matches are the big ones in September. When these exhibitions of orga-nized chaos are going on, everyone's attention is on them, so there isn't a lot of conversation. When the matches are over, though, the blabbing starts. The Irish are not a bit bashful and most have a standard opening to a chat: 1) "From the States then, are ye?" 2) "Enjoyin' yer holiday?" 3) "Have ye roots in Ireland, then?" This usually develops into a discussion of the difference in the weather between here and there. Most people in Ireland have only a faint concept about what and where Minnesota is, but nearly everyone has relatives in Boston or New York, and they some-times expected us to know them, being from the States and all.

Pubs are more social centres than places to get drunk. Actually on the whole trip, we only saw about a half a dozen people who were obviously loaded. The Irish drunk is pretty much a myth. We were treated every-where with warmth, courtesy, and informality. At one place I was having trouble identifying coins to pay for our drinks, so the young girl behind the bar just grabbed my hand and took out the right change.

So the preliminary pub-crawl was a success. I'll be adding pub infor-mation as we go along. We walked back to Belvedere about midnight to rest up for the epic salmon fishing expedition tomorrow.

A TERRIBLE HARD THING

SEPTEMBER 7. This is the day of the Great Salmon Expedition. Dan had introduced me to fly fishing some years back, I had been to Alaska several times and fished for salmon, and I'd had some success with rainbow trout in the Black Hills. When Dan and Tina spent their honeymoon in Ireland in 1996, they tried their hand at Atlantic salmon, so the old man had to try to one-up them. The River Moy runs right through Ballina and is reputed to be the finest salmon river in Ireland.

I had sent my fly rods to Doolin in August to avoid the hassle of carrying them on the plane. It was useful to have the Doolin post office right at the B&B so there wasn't any delivery problem. The rods were ready and waiting when we arrived.

The day dawned dark and rainy, but the weather in Ireland is so changeable that we didn't alter our plans. It would change five or six times before noon. We spent the morning writing postcards and catching up on the logbooks we were keeping. Nothing in Ireland opens before ten o'clock anyway.

As I see it, there is a good reason for this. Early in the morning, according to my learned theory, the pubs stack their empty barrels from the night before out on the curb. The Guinness truck comes around every morning straight from the brewery and replaces the empties with full ones. Now the streets in Irish towns are unbelievably narrow and crooked, and manoeuvring a semi loaded with beer barrels is a formidable task, even on an empty street. With traffic, it would be impossible. Therefore, everything waits until the pubs are supplied and the Guinness trucks have gone on their way. The alternative would be a national calamity. A pub running out of Guinness, and the delivery truck unable to get through? The shame of it all! There are songs about such catastrophes. But then the Irish have had centuries to work out sensible solutions to serious problems like this.

We walked downtown a little before ten to take care of a few business matters: changing money, mailing postcards, and arranging for fishing permits. A town the size of Ballina in the US would be spread out all over the place and walking would be inconvenient at best. In Ireland, every square inch is utilized, so a town is pretty compact. Walking from one end of Ballina to the other took only about twenty minutes. However, if you are planning out a schedule, you have to allow for conversation at every place you stop. I seldom saw an Irish person in a hurry, and most will strike up a conversation with you on the street.

We went first to a bank and exchanged money. We were delighted to see that the exchange rate was dropping dramatically by the day. We then walked across the River Moy on the old stone bridge to find the local fishing office. We couldn't locate it but we did find a branch post office to mail our cards. The place was tiny, about eight by ten feet, and seemed to have more employees than absolutely necessary, but the staff was very friendly. They asked the usual questions and chatted a bit. We asked about the location of the fishing office, and they told us that we had gone past it. It was down the street about a block back toward town on the other side of the street. Older Irish establishments generally don't have conspicuous markings on the outside, so we walked past the building and then back again until we spotted it. The sign on the door was about 4x6 inches.

Getting a fishing permit in Ireland is a real exercise in bureaucratic paperwork. The Irish may have kicked out the British, but they hung onto the English love of red tape. In the US, all you do is to go into a hardware store, pay your money and take your license. It's not that simple in Ireland. It requires a government issued license to fish for salmon, but not for trout. However, to fish anywhere for anything, you need a permit. Permits are issued by whoever owns the rights to a particular piece of shoreline. It could be a county or town government, national government, or a private landowner. The cost of a permit varies depending on the location of the "beat" (a section of shoreline) and its productivity. A beat may be a mile or so along a river or a hundred yards. Your permit allows you to fish for a certain time period only in the beat you have designated and paid for. Considering the honourable old Irish tradition of poaching, I wondered how well this was enforced.

We got all the information we needed (and there was a ton of it), and went to find a pub where we could examine it at our leisure. We walked back across the bridge, stopping to watch a few fishermen in the river. Most of them had chest waders and very long fly rods. We weren't so equipped and decided we'd look for a spot on the river where we could fish comfortably from the bank.

The pubs were now open (11AM) and we went into a pub just off the bridge: V.J. Dougherty's—Wine, Spirits, and Fishing Tackle. The only patrons present were two French guys at the bar. I knew they were French by the way they laughed. (They also spoke French.) All I could think was that somehow we had stumbled into Café Boeuf. Over a pint, we studied the maps we had gotten at the fishing office, weighed all the options, and picked out a spot on the map slightly upriver from the heart of town. There was a parking lot and a small park there and a walkway along the river.

We went back to the fishing office, filled out the forms, paid the fees for the beat we had selected, and started to head back to Belvedere to pick up our fishing equipment. As we were recrossing the bridge, we noticed a Renault dealership about a block away and figured this might be a good chance to see about getting our damaged wheel situation straightened out. We went in and told the manager what had happened.

He didn't seem very surprised and told us that he most likely could take care of it. It seems that hitting rocks and bashing up wheels is an everyday occurrence. In fact, our hostess, Mary Reily, had done the very same thing a few days ago on the road to Castlebar. The manager asked us if we had insurance and I told him I did, but it was a £250 deductible policy and if I took it back to Avis, they would probably decide that the damage was at least that much. He said he could do better and to bring the car in later.

After stopping at another fishing shop where the clerk sold me some flies that were guaranteed salmon killers, we went back to Belvedere, took everything out of the boot and drove back down to the Renault dealer. I drove Clio into the shop and was impressed by the way the lads went to work. They replaced the rim, put the tyre back on it and then drove me up the street to a tyre shop to have the replacement checked and cleaned, drove back to the dealership, cleaned and dried the spare, put on a new wheel cover and a factory type seal, and washed out any trace of a mishap. I guessed that they saw this as a chance to strike a blow against a giant oppressor (Avis) and to save the downtrodden (me) from a potential screwing. I thanked them all profusely for their help, and was handed a bill, with a grin and the statement "That'll fix the bastards," for the sum of only £50.

We went over to our selected fishing spot and got at it. Micki quit after a half-hour, and started exploring around the area, taking videotape and still pictures. I stuck with it for a couple of hours, but there wasn't any action. The locals weren't having any luck either.

It was nearly the end of the season, so I guess I shouldn't have expected much. Still, it was a pleasant experience. People were going back and forth on the walkway behind us and sometimes stopping to see how things were going. A priest came along and sat down on a bench to take in a little sun. I thought he'd try for a little divine intervention on my behalf, but I guess God doesn't help out with fishing.

One guy came stomping up the riverbank and came right up to me with a deadly serious look on his face. I thought I might be breaking some regulation or breaching some kind of fishing etiquette, but he just pronounced in sepulchral tones, "A terrible hard thing it is to catch the salmon," and plodded mournfully on his way up the river. I guess that made us brother losers.

Even though we didn't catch anything, it was satisfying to spend the afternoon away from the tourist trail and just do what the natives do at a leisurely Irish pace, not at American warp speed.

Our evening was another memorable pub-crawl. There were several pubs that we had missed the night before, so we had to take up the slack before we left County Mayo. Our first stop was the Parting Glass.

Now herein lies a tale of innocents abroad. Micki had seen somewhere in an ad that this place "specializes" in cocktails. The Parting Glass is quite small and a little worn, but comfortable. The most striking thing about it is the American Indian decor. There are portraits of Sitting Bull, Geronimo, Chief Joseph and several others hanging on the walls; maps and other Native American artefacts are displayed all over the place. When we sat down at the bar and asked for a cocktail menu, the young guy behind the bar handed Micki a list of "Sex on the Beach," "Screaming Orgasm," and a few other syrupy exotic sounding concoctions. Micki decided to have a "What the Hell." The barman got a little flustered and started rummaging around under the bar looking for the ingredients. After a few minutes, a lady came back behind the bar and asked him what he was looking for. He couldn't find lemon juice. The lady handed him a bottle of Rose's sweetened limejuice and said in a very stagy whisper, "Here. She'll never know the difference." The result was a fruity concoction with one ice cube and a little paper umbrella in it.

The lady who got the limejuice gave a clue to the décor. She had very distinctive Native American features, but how she ended up in Ballina is anybody's guess. I wasn't about to ask for fear I'd probably find out at great length and in great detail. Hearing her talk was just a little disconcerting: Sacajawea with a brogue.

The Reilys had recommended dinner at Tullio's, a restaurant in the heart of Ballina. We took their suggestion and weren't disappointed. Micki tried once more to get an American style cocktail and ordered a Martini. This turned out to be a tall glass of dry white vermouth over ice with a lemon wedge. So much for creeping Americanisation. The dinner was superb though. Micki had a venison roast with red currant sauce, and I had a mixed seafood grill. I didn't recognize some of the fish, but it was all delicious.

We went across the street to Hogan's for an after-dinner Paddy, the most popular brand of Irish whiskey. In the short time I'd been here, I'd gotten pretty fond of it. There were some college age kids in Hogan's watching an Irish version of "Who Wants To Be A Millionaire?" on television. Having gotten used to pub manners by now, we joined in with them. These kids were really into the game, cheering and booing and calling out answers. We gave a few and they liked that. One question involved fluorine and chlorine. The correct answer was "halogens." I whispered it to the young girl sitting next to me and she yelled it out. Her friends asked her how she knew that. She told them, "The Yank told me," and gave me a high five. Apparently, it was refreshing for them to see two old Americans on their own in a pub, and not part of an overly supervised tour.

After the quiz show, "East Enders" came on. Maybe you've seen it on PBS. It's a running soap opera about poor Londoners with scraggly hair and bad teeth. Tonight's episode had to do with an old lady who has been taking her last breath for the last couple of months, and tonight someone is giving her a birthday cake. The college kids quieted down immediately and got very engrossed. I was about to make a smart-ass remark, but I noticed that these kids were taking it very seriously, and wisely decided to keep my mouth shut. The cake sequence lasted about 15 minutes, and when it was over, this big kid farther down the bar wiped his eyes and sighed, "Jaysus, Mary, and sweet Joseph!" I tried to detect some hint of sarcasm here, but I couldn't. If these kids weren't serious, it was the most well staged put-on I've ever seen.

We then went up the street to the Crescent, a little pub with about eight barstools. The barman, a young guy named Eamon, started with the usual inquiries about our holiday. He was pretty talkative and gave us some 30-second history: "Did you know the Waterboys sat on those very stools not even a month ago? Indeed, the very spot it was." He also recommended that we stay in Letterkenny, County Donegal, instead of Donegal Town, as we had planned for tomorrow night. Before we left, he showed us a few parlour tricks to entertain our friends at home. One involved making a full glass of Guinness stick to a wall.

We left Mr. Information and visited two more pubs on the way home, quiet little places to just sit a while in. The last place, Paddy Jordan's seemed to be the hangout for folks our age. They were supposed to have traditional music that night, but the musicians apparently didn't show up. We got home at 11:30 and crashed. It had been a pretty full day.

THINGS ARE DIFFERENT UP HERE

SEPTEMBER 8. Breakfast at the Reilys was superb, as we have come to expect even in the short time we have been here. Mary booked us into a B&B in Letterkenny, County Donegal, for our evening's accommodations. We had originally intended to stop in Donegal town, but Eamon the barman at the Crescent last night suggested that Letterkenny had better pubs and night life. One of the travel brochures we had obtained declared that in Donegal, things are different. We were looking forward to finding out.

We packed up Clio, making sure that we had the pack of brochures that Mary wanted us to drop off at our next stop. We started north and within ten minutes discovered we were on the wrong road. We turned around, went back to Ballina, found the right road and headed for Sligo. We had a bunch of maps, but most of them were too vague for our needs, so we did a lot of backtracking.

We arrived in Sligo at 11:30 and gassed up for the first time. Clio was getting about 43 mpg and figuring out the current exchange rate and converting to American gallons, we were paying $3.15/ gallon. Pretty stiff by American standards, but not as bad as I thought it was going to be.

About five miles north of Sligo is Drumcliffe, a small village in whose Protestant churchyard W.B.Yeats is buried. We had to stop and pay homage to the memory of that strange and mystical voice of the Celtic Revival.

Yeats' beloved Benbulben overlooks the church, and on viewing the mysterious flat-topped mountain, I could understand Yeats' fascination. Legends about Benbulben are numerous and ancient. One states that Diarmuid, the ancient Celtic hero, is buried somewhere on its slopes. Another says that if a person spends a night on the mountain and comes back alive, he will thereafter have either magic powers or complete madness.

The churchyard itself is very peaceful and serene. It's very Church of Ireland and looks a lot like what you'd imagine the Anglo-Irish gentry would frequent: in Ireland, but somehow separate from the surrounding countryside. Just strolling around in the cemetery was a very calming and meditative experience. We, of course, took pictures of Yeats' gravestone with its memorable epitaph, and just soaked up the atmosphere.

The mood was broken when the tour buses started to arrive. The people getting off obviously hadn't a clue as to why they were there. Most of them headed for the gift shop to buy green ashtrays or plastic shamrocks. We knew it was time to leave when some German guy asked Micki, "Who vass diss Yeets, anyvay?" At least he was interested enough to ask.

The drive toward Donegal was very scenic. The roads were in much better shape. We took N15 through a small chunk of County Leitrim through Bundoran and into County Donegal to Ballyshannon and then to Donegal town.

Donegal is a small town of 2300 and is a nightmare of crooked streets, but it's quite picturesque. We found a parking place without too much difficulty and strolled the town for a while. A powerful thirst had come upon us, and we found a pub right away, not a really tough task, since there's usually a pub every 50 feet in most towns. Jimmy's Pub was about 15 feet from our parking space so we went in. It was extremely small and shabby, but with a whole bar full of Barry Fitzgerald types. We were in Ulster now and the accent is often unintelligible, so there wasn't too much conversation we could get into.

We walked across the street to a pub whose name I don't remember. We were looking for some lunch and thought they might serve food in here. There was nobody in the place except one guy at the bar who was pretty loaded. He was very talkative and seemed to think that we were going to sit down and catch up with his present state. Spending an afternoon getting sloshed with an Irish drunk wasn't very appealing, so we bid our farewells to him with as much courtesy as we could muster.

We headed down the hill to the town square and into McGroarty's to have a bite. Micki had a huge grilled sandwich and I had a sort of fish plate—batter-fried haddock chunks and roasted potatoes, not your lite luncheon for healthy arteries, but really tasty and filling.

Up the street back towards our car was an outlet shop for Donegal tweeds and yarn. Micki loaded up on yarn for making sweaters and arranged to have it shipped home. I had to buy a Donegal tweed cap that I thought was pretty cool. I thought it would make me look a little more native. It didn't, of course, but that little bit of self-delusion was comforting.

We left Donegal and headed for Letterkenny. Again the roads were in good shape and the scenery was spectacular. The highway went through one brilliantly green valley after another. The smooth slopes of the surrounding mountains changed with every curve.

Letterkenny is a town of 7000 and is situated at the mouth of Lough Swilly in a very lovely valley. Our B&B, Town View, was on the south side of town on a hill over looking the valley, the cathedral, the River Swilly, and MacDonald's Golden Arches. We had no trouble finding it, since there was a series of signs posted every hundred feet showing the direction to Town View B&B. It was off the beaten path in a quiet residential neighborhood, with the inevitable sheep and cows in the pasture next door. We found that in Ireland, just as you're never out of sight of a pub, you're never out of sight of sheep and cows either.

Town View is owned by Dan and May Herrity. After the usual introductory question about where we were from, May asked us if we were familiar with Cushing, Minnesota. Cushing is a little town about 40 miles from our home in Melrose, and we are quite familiar with the place. We were surprised that someone in Ireland was that familiar with Minnesota geography, but it seems that the manager of the Super 8 motel in Cushing is from Letterkenny and used to stay at Town View on his visits home. Surprising little bit of the world wide web of human acquaintances.

May gave us some brochures on things to do in Letterkenny and gave us directions on walking to town. "Keep the cathedral in front of you, you can't get lost." That last statement was always a negative self-fulfilling prophecy: when anybody told us we couldn't get lost, we invariably did.

We started down the hill, and since there's no such thing as a straight street or square corner in Ireland, we ended up in a little residential cul-de-sac. There were two little guys about 8 or 9 years old on the street fooling around with hurling sticks. (No hockey sticks or baseball bats here.) The two of them could have been stand-ins for *Angela's Ashes*: freckles, pug noses, and oversized ears. When we turned around to backtrack, we got questioned: "Y'lost then? Are y'travelin'? Where y'frum?" What seems like nosiness to Americans is just ordinary conversation to the Irish, even kids.

We got straightened out in short order and belatedly remembered the signs pointing out the direction to Town View. Getting back would be much simpler. The Herritys must have figured out Americans' inclination to get lost.

Downtown Letterkenny is the usual labyrinth, with its satisfying complement of pubs. We went into the Metropolitan Hotel as May had recommended. This was a pretty upscale place with a large bar. There was actually excess space! We sat at the bar, had a pint and ordered our dinner. Micki had lamb ravioli and I had the Cumberland sausage and mash. This was a big heap of mashed potatoes with a spiral of sausage coiled on top and drizzled with gravy. It looked like a dead snake or a dog pile, but looks not withstanding, it was delicious. The sausage was spicy, but not overpowering. I'm going to have to find the recipe and try to duplicate it.

Full to the gills, we went out on the street to survey the pub scene. Eamon was right: there is no shortage of pubs in Letterkenny. The first one we went into was Nellie's, a fairly large place, but pretty empty except for a guy at one end of the bar and two English women, who were about to leave. Listening to them, the adjective "dotty" leapt to mind. They looked like the type who own thirty five cats and putter around in a herb garden all day, and then go out on a "Save the Squirrels" rally. They had been calling the young barman "Milord" and apparently thinking that this was very funny, told us that we should also. The barman had a vague artificial smile pasted on his face, as he listened to their crap. They finally left, and the smile turned into a grimace of disgust. When they were well out the door, the guy at the end of the bar said something. I didn't get it all, but I did catch something like "fookin' English. What can y'expect?"

We left Nellie's and visited a couple more places, mostly young folks' hangouts. We made an attempt to call home from a phone booth, but we didn't have the international code for the US, so that didn't work.

Our last stop was the Drum, a tiny place with 8 barstools. You have to get the picture here. The bar was L-shaped with three stools on the short leg and five on the long side. A couple about our age were sitting on the short side and three guys were sitting at the long side, leaving a couple of empty stools on the corner. We took those, ordered, and listened in on the conversation between the couple on our left and the three guys on the right. We had found out that you really don't have to be formally invited into a conversation in a pub; if you are there, you are automatically involved. We were in the middle of a current discussion about the state of roads in Ireland. The couple on the left were from Scotland and were discussing the easiest way to return to Belfast tomorrow to catch the ferry home. The guys on the right weren't much help partly because we couldn't understand them and also because they couldn't agree on the best route. The girl behind the bar got out a road map and the problem was shortly solved to everyone's satisfaction.

In a few minutes, the young girl left and was replaced by an older lady. She asked us where we were from, and when we told her, she was delighted and pointed out an old Miller High Life mirror on the wall. Several years ago, a tourist from Minnesota had been in the Drum and enjoyed himself so much that he promised to send a memento. The lady said that she never expected him to really do it. She was surprised and gratified when the mirror arrived intact. It's been on the wall ever since.

The conversation eventually got around to the universal bar topic: drinking. When the local guy who did most of the talking found out we were Americans, he said that he had heard that in Louisiana it was legal to distill your own liquor. I told him I didn't think so, but that probably quite a few people did and didn't get caught. It was generally agreed that liquor laws anywhere were intolerably oppressive and trampled on the natural rights of man. Remember that this is an area where every other farmer probably has a *poitín* still in his barn.

We were also informed that once you left the Republic, the Guinness is inferior. It simply does not taste right, begod, once you're out of the country, and this includes Northern Ireland. Jesus, Mary and Joseph! We'll be in Derry tomorrow, and besides the risk of getting shot, we won't even be able to get a decent pint!

To get the full impact of what follows, you have to imagine this: the Scottish guy looked like a heavy Richard Harris and had a dead-on Sean Connery voice: teeth clenched, growly, but articulate. The conversation got around to occupations, and I asked Sean Connery what he did. I found out later that asking people about their work is considered rude, but the Scot didn't seem to mind. He was a retired woodworking teacher. I told him I used to be a teacher and asked him what he taught. He replied in the greatest Highlander Jacobite *Sassenach*-hating accent: "A boonch of bloody leetle bahstards!" The *craic* was getting mighty.

I felt like having a scotch and asked for a brand on the back bar that I'd never seen before. The Scot got a faint look of disgust on his face and remarked that he himself wouldn't touch that stuff and of course pro-ceeded to tell us why. He lives and apparently worked very close to a dis-tillery in Scotland and often did custom woodworking for them. One time the distillery asked him to repair a wooden wheel on a horse drawn wagon they kept for publicity purposes. He was asked to use oak from some old aging barrels they had. The oak was so permeated with Scotch that he swore that he got drunk sniffing the sawdust. Since then, he hasn't touched a drop of it.

We eventually got around to his favorite topic of salmon and trout fishing. Now a Celt with an audience can get into high gear pretty fast and when he's on his favorite topic, there's no stopping him. The Scot told us that he lives on a river and can fish anytime he wants even though he doesn't have fishing rights. He can cast from his back yard across the strip of bank where the fishing rights are designated. Since he is technically not on the bank, he can get away with it. He only keeps trophy trout, but his neighbors catch trash fish and sell them to the English because they (the English) don't know any better. A general round of agreement followed that one.

We left the Drum full of Scotch (me anyway) and managed to find our way home without difficulty. It had been another pretty full day.

1608 AND BEYOND

SEPTEMBER 9. This is the day we take a great leap into the unknown: crossing over into Northern Ireland. With all the stuff on the news about the violence, we were not sure what to expect. I wanted to see for myself what, if anything, was going on.

The breakfast was the usual tasty feast. May wondered if there was anybody left in the US; they all seemed to be in Ireland. She also mentioned that in August the place was full of Italians, apparently escaping the heat. "And they are a noisy bunch!"

Before checking out, we asked May to book us a place in Ballymena that we had picked out. The lady in Ballymena told May there was no way anybody could get a place that night because a big flower show was going on. May suggested stopping at a tourist information office someplace. They usually can find a place for you.

It's only about 30 minutes drive, even at our pace, to the border. At least I think so. Actually, there was no indication of crossing a line at all. The only way we could tell we had crossed was that we started seeing the Union Jack instead of the Republic's tricolour. I had somewhat expected Checkpoint Charlie type stations on the border with barbed wire and combat troops searching the car. No such thing. So much for CNN and telling the truth.

We passed through the outskirts of Londonderry rather quickly. (Catholics call the city and county Derry, Protestants call them Londonderry, but we didn't call them anything aloud, trying to keep neutrality.) I was expecting to see barricades on streets, patrolling tanks and armoured cars, and the air filled with bricks and Molotov cocktails. Instead, what we saw was a clean, modern city with well-marked and well-surfaced streets, trees, boulevards, and flower-beds. So much for the Irish-American press and telling the whole truth.

I will say this: the roads in Northern Ireland are a lot better on average than in the Republic—wider and better paved, and better marked. Driving in the countryside beyond Londonderry wasn't a lot different than driving through Minnesota or Wisconsin.

We made a stop at Limavady, a really pretty town, to do our business: change money, book a place for the night, and check out the Guinness. Banks were closed, but we had Sterling in travellers' checks so that wasn't a big problem. The local tourist office was closed, so we'd have to take care of that elsewhere. The pubs were open, so we went into the Roebuck Inn for a pint of research. The guy in Letterkenny was right—it doesn't taste the same. Guinness here tastes more like the stuff you get in the US.

Limavady is the place where "Danny Boy" originated. The story goes (and in Ireland there is a story about everything) that a lady in the 18th century, Jane Ross, heard the melody being played by an itinerant fiddler as he passed beneath her window. She was so impressed by the beauty of the tune that she wrote it down. The air became popular and was generally known as the Londonderry Air. Words were composed for it and the song is now universally known and instantly recognized as "Danny Boy." There is a big memorial in front of a building commemorating the song. It was pretty amateurish, looking like it had been done as a grade school project, but it was kind of cute.

We headed for Coleraine, enroute to the famed Giant's Causeway. Coleraine is a fairly charming town, with the usual crooked streets and crazy arrangement of buildings. We found the tourist office without too much difficulty and got ourselves booked into a B&B at Ballymoney, not too far away.

The computerized booking system known as Gulliver in both the Republic and Northern Ireland is amazing. Nearly all tourist accommodations are listed in the tourist office computers. All a traveller has to do is tell the office staff the destination for the evening, the type of accommodation, and preferred location in the community. All possibilities are downloaded with particulars about the place—cost, amenities, distance from attractions and other pertinent information. The tourist picks out his preference and the tourist office calls the place to see if there are any openings. If there are openings, reservations are made on the spot, and the lodgings are waiting. If there are no openings, another choice can be made. Once a reservation is made, there is a small fee of £2 to pay for the phone call. Since tourist offices are frequent all over Ireland, making reservations is very simple.

Just outside of Coleraine is Portrush (reputedly a place where blowing up cars and buildings is a local sport), and the Giant's Causeway. This is an incredible chunk of coastline, well worth a couple of hours' visit. It's the remains of an ancient volcanic eruption that cooled off into pillars of basalt in nearly perfect hexagonal columns. The tops of the columns resemble paving stones. That's the scientific explanation. I prefer the one in which Fionn MacCumhail built a roadway for his giant Scottish sweetheart to cross over to Ireland.

For those who wanted, buses ran to the various scenic spots. We walked instead, scoffing at the effete tourists who were half our age and didn't have the stamina to walk. Alongside the path, blackberry bushes were all over the hillside. The berries were ripe and quite a few tourists (including us) stopped and picked a small lunch right off the bushes. No need to worry about disturbing the ecosystem. In Ireland, blackberries (known there as brambles) are considered weeds.

I found a piece of driftwood along the shore that looked like it may have been part of a boat. I picked it up and brought it home to my five-year-old granddaughter Katie and told her it was from the ship of Sorley MacDonald, a famous Antrim pirate in the 17th century. She was thrilled with it. I told her about McDonald and his eerie castle at Dunluce, a few miles away from the Causeway. She loved the story about how part of the castle fell into the sea, and she has more or less adopted Sorley as her personal pirate.

About two miles from the Giant's Causeway is one of the truly holy shrines in all of Ireland: **BUSHMILL'S DISTILLERY!** We had the option of a guided tour through the operations part of the distillery or were free to just walk around the place. After looking at the people lining up for tour tickets, who didn't look like they knew good whiskey from Listerine, we opted for the wandering around.

Bushmill's has been in continuous operation since the thirteenth century and licensed since 1608. The place is like a time warp. If it weren't for the trucks parked around, you'd think it really was 1608. There is an excellent gift shop and a fantastic tasting room. The tasting is free, with apparently no limit, except your own commonsense. Other brands besides the Bushmill's varieties are available, and we sampled several types that aren't available in the US. Great experience: it opened up a whole new world of snobbery.

I could have sat there for the rest of the day, but we did let sense prevail. I didn't want to run into the RUC driving with a skinful. I wear a medal blessed by the Pope, and Micki carries a rosary. Getting caught driving drunk with these little Papist artifacts might get us an introduction to the internment camp at Long Kesh. ("Free the Minnesota Two!")

Ballymoney isn't too far from Bushmill's, maybe a twenty-minute drive. We found our B&B without any difficulty. Hob Green, run by Brian and Jean Johnston, is on several acres just outside of Ballymoney.

Brian is quite a gardener and has the place landscaped to perfection. It's one of those English-type gardens with pools and little walks that seem to lead nowhere, but are all very thoughtfully laid out. When we rang the bell, Brian came to the door looking like he'd been doing some heavy-duty gardening. He was wearing old clothes, work gloves, and a good deal of garden dirt. When I pointed out a caterpillar crawling on his shirt, he gingerly removed it and carried it gently outside and put it on a shrub, and then showed us to our room looking out over a pasture and a wide view of a very green valley beyond.

We had supper that evening in Ballymoney at Kelly's Taproom and Cellar, a place owned by Jean Johnston's brother. I had a sirloin and Micki had a prawn and potato cake dish. All very good.

On the way back to the car, we spotted a phone booth, so we called home. You can get a phone card nearly anywhere and the phone system in Ireland, both parts, is very good.

The phone booth was right next to the Ballymoney taxi stand. (They call it a "rank.") While Micki was on the phone, an argument broke out between two drivers about hogging parking space. We found out a few days later that taxis are favourite targets for firebombs. Until the argument subsided, I was ready to tuck and roll.

We got back to Hob Green at 9PM and called it quits. It had been a memorable day: we saw a good deal of the country, we didn't collect any bullet holes, and we didn't get lost. Quite a list of accomplishments.

A BOREEN GREEN

SEPTEMBER 10. We had a slight shift in the breakfast routine this morning. Instead of the usual Irish breakfast, Micki had French toast and bacon (the Irish variety, of course) and I had kippers and scrambled eggs. Since we were technically in the UK and kippers seem so very British, I thought it would be appropriate. Micki thought they reeked up the house, but Brian and Jean seemed pleased. We were the only guests at Hob Green that day, so the breakfast was leisurely and casual. Brian and Jean are quite chatty and friendly, so we lingered over our breakfast talking with them.

Jean asked us if we were tracing our roots, as so many Americans do. We said we weren't, but we both did have roots in the area. Jean commented that tracing one's roots is a foreign idea to the Irish, since their roots are right where they are—they've never been anyplace else.

The conversation drifted a bit toward the Troubles. Brian didn't say much about it, except "we get an awful lot of bad press." I didn't pursue it, so I don't know exactly whom he meant by "we." He may have meant the province as a whole, or whatever party he belonged to. I assumed he was Protestant, since County Antrim is almost 100% Protestant, but somehow I couldn't picture him as a member of any kind of hate group; he wouldn't even kill a caterpillar. Maybe I missed a chance to get some valid insights, but then again, I wasn't there to investigate and draw conclusions. They've had enough of that from outsiders.

In Northern Ireland, the national highways are designated "A" roads, and the secondary roads are designated "B" routes. We left Ballymoney at 10:00 and headed south on A26 toward Ballymena and Antrim town. Around Ballymena, A26 briefly turns into M2. The M designation indicates a "limited access dual carriageway." We'd call it a freeway. This is the first time we'd run into a four-lane highway, and the increase in speed was amazing. M routes work just like our interstates, except that ramps move toward the left.

In a gloomy misting rain, we drove through Antrim town, where my grandmother was born. My grandmother, Elizabeth Welsh, came to America at age twelve escorting two younger siblings. (Talk about unaccompanied minors!) She was sent to relatives in Massachusetts because her parents feared for her life in the old Ulster battle between Protestants and Catholics. She bore a scar on her forehead her entire life, the result of the rage of a Protestant woman whacking her with a shovel for having the audacity to play with Protestant kids. I had this little bit of family myth in my mind when we drove through Antrim.

It could be that my imagination was getting out of hand, but it seemed to reek of Orange Order. It was Sunday and there was little traffic. Maybe they were all in church, selling tickets to a Pope-effigy kicking contest. I don't know.

We kept following A26 until it joined M1 and turned east for 7 or 8 miles. Just outside of Lisburn, we got onto A1, the main Belfast-Dublin road. A26 is not an M route, but it is a "dual carriageway," that is, a four-lane highway. We were making very good time. Somewhere along here, we spotted a "layby," what we would call a rest stop. It wasn't much, just a small parking lot on the side of the road. We pulled off for a bit of a stretch and a look around. There was a small path leading off through a patch of woods, so I suggested that Micki pose on it and I'd take her picture. You know the old song, "The Star of the County Down:"

> "Near Banbridge town in the County Down
> One morning last July,
> On a boreen green was a fair colleen,
> And she smiled as she passed me by."

We kept going south past Dromore and Banbridge to the border town of Newry. Since it was now 12:30 and pubs were open, we stopped for a last pint of research before leaving Ulster. The town seemed pretty deserted, so we had no trouble finding parking. There were no other cars in the parking lot, and I got the uneasy feeling that there might be a bomb ticking away somewhere in the area.

We walked a few blocks to the Quayside Inn, and had a pint. Sure enough, it was Northern Ireland Guinness. We sat for a while and watched a young kid waiting tables who could have been Liam Neeson's younger brother. We considered asking him if he was, but thought better of it.

As we were walking back to the car, we saw the first tangible evidence of the Ulster situation: There was razor wire strung in menacing coils across alleyways and rooftops. In spite of the Good Friday Agreement, the Troubles are alive and active. We found out later that a fleet of taxis had been torched the night before in Armagh, about 15 miles away.

Newry is about five miles from the border, but the border's exact location on the road is rather vague. No checkpoints here either. At 1:45PM, we arrived in Dundalk, where the main industry is the brewing of Harp Lager and Kaliber non-alcoholic beer. We were now back in the Republic far sooner than we had anticipated. We had booked a B&B here and they weren't expecting us until around 5, so we walked around and sampled a few pubs.

We went into the Clanbrassil Hotel, got our pints and sat down in the lobby/lounge. There was a bunch of young guys in there singing some old 60's American doo-wop songs, and butchering them pretty badly.

They didn't care; they were enjoying themselves and thought we were too. They got up after awhile and headed out, not without shaking hands all around and wishing us a good day.

A guy and his wife and ten-year-old son joined us and started to tell us about an open-air market just back across the border in Ulster. They were from Newry, and every Sunday they drive down to Dundalk for dinner at the hotel and a stop at the market for bargains. The leather jacket he was wearing only cost £5. He also told us there were some terrific bargains on electronics there too: software, cassette and CD players and the like, no doubt pirated. I was thinking about "yalla-headed tinkers" and swift disappearances when the police show up, but he didn't say anything about that, so I didn't either.

There were two guys asleep on couches in the lobby, and the manager was trying to get them out of there. One woke up and tried to get his buddy up, but failed so he just shrugged and walked out.

We said goodbye to the folks from Newry and left the Clanbrassil. We wandered down the street and around the corner into the Tara. Wolfe-Tones rebel songs were blaring on the jukebox and the place was full of late teen guys in leather jackets. Dundalk has the reputation of being an IRA staging point, and I guessed that this was one of the hangouts. I could well imagine this bunch running up across the border and stirring up a little turmoil. The guy that woke up in the hotel lobby wandered in and joined the crowd.

At that point we felt a little uneasy, so we drank up, left, and went across the street to Moe's Bar. The place is a sort of sports bar and there was a hurling match on TV. This was the first time I'd paid much attention to the game and wasn't following it too well. From what I could tell, it looked pretty brutal.

We had seen advertising along the way for a new Guinness product: Breó (pronounced "Bro"). We decided that three weeks of beer sampling wouldn't be complete without giving it a try. It's not too bad. It's a light coloured tart beer with a definite citrus tang, much like Belgian Witbier.

After leaving Moe's, we walked back to where we parked and headed for our evening's accommodations. We found our B&B after a few sidetracks. Following Irish street and house numbers is an exercise in futility, and trying to follow verbal directions isn't much better. We did stumble onto the place though. It's called Krakow (I've no idea why. I thought we were in Ireland, not Poland.) and run by Larry and Marian Witherow, who kindly sent us a St. Patrick's Day card the following March.

The room was adequate, if a little odd. The walls were a sort of blazing pink, and the bathroom was sponged with blotches of deep red, to match the solid red toilet seat with an owl on the underside of the lid. It was a tiny room with a Ward & June arrangement. (Our term for twin beds. You remember the Cleavers and their very chaste marital arrangements on American TV in the fifties?) However, it was clean and quiet.

At 7:00, we headed back downtown for dinner. We took a few wrong turns, but we were getting resigned to the fact that the day wasn't complete without getting lost at least once. Dundalk is a city of 30,000, and in a town that size getting a few blocks off isn't a major disaster.

We ate at Padraig O'Donnegail's Bar-Lounge and Restaurant. It was an interesting little place, with a lot of little nooks and crannies. The toilets were out the back door and a few paces down the alley. By this time, we'd quit asking why about a lot of arrangements in Ireland. You just do what the Irish do.

Our dining area was a small room off the bar section. The menu was pretty extensive and interesting. We followed our usual procedure of staying with items that seemed distinctively Irish. Micki had venison with whiskey sauce, and I had chicken stuffed with smoked salmon and shrimp. Both were delicious.

We shared the dining area with a young couple. She was an attractive young lady about 20 and had the classic 60's look: white eye shadow, pencilled eyebrows, and bell-bottom jeans. I didn't know whether this was retro-cool or that Dundalk was thirty years behind the times.

We stopped for an after dinner drink at the Central, a little quiet pub without too much to distinguish it, and then found our way back to Krakow with only a little difficulty and got a sound sleep to prepare for the trip to Dublin tomorrow.

OUT OF THE MISTS OF TIME

SEPTEMBER 11. This is the day we head for Dublin. The black and white puddings for breakfast were a little different tasting than usual, more like German blood sausage, but we learned there are as many varieties of this stuff as there are Irish butchers. As he served breakfast, our host Larry gave us some tips on driving to Dublin. His main point was "Don't go there." He warned us that traffic would be heavy, as it was a Monday; there would be a lot of trucks on the road ("heavy lorries"); that we shouldn't drive in the city of Dublin; and if we did, don't park illegally, because if you do, your car gets towed and it costs £100 to get it back, even if you are American. He injected "you know" pretty frequently into the conversation.

He did tell us though that if we were really determined to head to Dublin, not to miss the prehistoric tombs at Newgrange, which are right on the way. My concept of Irish geography is sometimes a little vague, and I hadn't realized that Newgrange was that close to our route. We were grateful for the tip.

A1 in the North becomes N1 in the republic and is a dual carriageway most of the time. Newgrange is right outside of Drogheda, so we stopped and asked for directions. The guy at a petrol station said it was well marked, and all we had to do was cross the bridge just ahead of us, turn left and go about a mile until we saw a McDonald's on the left. He stopped and said, "You know what a McDonald's looks like?" Then he saw "American" all over me and said, "Oh, of course you do. Just turn right at that corner and you'll drive right to it."

His directions were good, and we found the road all right, but it was neither an N road nor an R road. It was an "other," which in Irish means goats are afraid of it. However, tour buses full of solemn Japanese seem to manage, so we gave it a try. Once we got to the site, however, there was a big modern visitor centre with ample parking.

Newgrange is a large complex of Neolithic (Late Stone Age) tombs spread out over several miles in the Boyne Valley. The visitor centre is actually several miles away from the tombs, so there is a procedure for visiting. You purchase a ticket at the centre, then walk across a foot-bridge over the River Boyne. We stopped on the footbridge for a few moments to see if it is true that "Clear is the water that flows from the Boyne." The water was clear but of a sort of tea-coloured shade, probably picked up from the miles of peat bogs it flows through.

Several hundred yards down a path is a spot where a bus picks you up and drives to the site itself. You have a choice of visiting Newgrange or either of the other two sites: Knowth or Dowth. Once there, a college kid conducts a foot tour with explanations of the site. When you're finished, the bus takes you back to the pickup spot, and you walk back to the visitor centre.

The tomb at Newgrange is a massive mound of stone and earth approximately 250 feet in diameter. As far as anyone knows, it was built as a tomb and monument for some very important people somewhere around 3500 BC (long before Stonehenge and the pyramids). There is evidence around the site of a large, and apparently prosperous, community. The perimeter of the mound is a series of nearly identically sized boulders, each measuring about 3x3x10 feet in size. Many of them are carved with mysterious patterns of spirals, circles, and diamond shapes. Above this foundation is a twenty-foot high facing of white quartz interspersed with grey stone.

There is an opening on the southeast face of the mound that leads to a passage about sixty feet long. The passage is constructed with upright slabs of stone on the sides and covered over with horizontal slabs. The walls and the ceiling are covered with the same patterns found outside on the foundation boulders.

At the end of the passage is a domed chamber nineteen feet high at the centre, with three smaller chambers leading off from it in a cross shaped arrangement. The dome of the main chamber uses a construction technique called corbelling, a series of overlapping stone slabs that gradually form the dome. The side chambers are similarly constructed and are the heart of the structure. In each of the recesses rests a large finely shaped stone basin, in which human remains have been found.

Engineers and archaeologists have surmised that the passage, the main chamber, and its adjoining recesses were constructed as a free-standing structure within the circumference of the foundation boulders. When it was finished, the whole thing was covered with earth and rock to complete the huge mound as it stands today.

As if the structure itself weren't inspiring enough, there's more. Above the outside entrance to the passageway, there is a rectangular opening about 2½ x 3¼ feet in size. No one could figure out the purpose of this opening, called the roof box, until 1967, when Professor M.J. O'Kelly of the University College Cork, discovered its secret: the passage is aligned so precisely that at sunrise on the winter solstice, a ray of sunlight travels along the ceiling of the passage and eventually illuminates the burial chambers. The illumination lasts about fifteen minutes, and then as the sun rises higher, the light ray recedes back down the floor of the passage and leaves the chamber in total darkness for another year.

The visitors that day at Newgrange were given some basic information about the site and then were free to walk around the grounds and examine the exterior walls and foundation stones. Given the Irish sense of drama, this was probably an intentional prelude for the next stage of the tour.

We were divided up into groups of about fifteen and told we would now be taken into the interior of the tomb. We were warned by the young lady guiding us that the footing inside was uneven, and that the passage was narrow and dark. If anyone was claustrophobic, perhaps they should not go in.

We entered the passage lit only by the guide's flashlight. The passage inclines upward toward the burial chambers and narrows down at times to only about two feet wide by five feet high. The physical effect, though, wasn't half as powerful as the psychological effect. We were leaving the modern world completely behind, and the farther we progressed up the passage, the more we could feel the presence of those ancient people. The mysterious carvings all around us gave everyone in the group the feeling that there was something more here than an interesting but primitive pile of stone. Each step of the way dropped us back a century in time, and by the time we reached the main chamber with its dimly lit side recesses, the twenty-first century had disappeared and we were in a place and time way beyond our understanding.

The guide gave us some time to examine the recesses off the main chamber. These were like small rooms, each with a stone basin originally containing funeral remains. The three-foot hand carved basins were as smooth and regular as if they had been machined; amazing craftsmanship, considering people without metal tools made them.

After we had examined the recesses, the guide explained the winter solstice phenomenon and then turned off all the lights. When we were in total darkness, she then told us that she would turn on an electric simulation of the solstice light. There was a pause, and then a ray of light started travelling across the ceiling of the passage toward us and eventually reached the chamber and gradually lit up the entire room. The carvings on the dome became visible and the side recesses were illuminated. As the light ray reached its greatest strength, there was a collective gasp from the whole group. I don't think it was only the beauty of it, although that was considerable, but the realization that these highly intelligent, inventive and energetic people at Newgrange 5000 years ago were very real, they had left their mark for all time, and that for a brief moment, we modern people from all over the world had become part of them.

After the light ray had receded back down the floor of the passage, the guide led us back toward the entrance. There was very little conversation on the way back. The whole group was pretty quiet. For a few minutes there, we had been in what the ancient Celts called a "thin place," where ordinary time and space disappear, and stepping into another world is possible.

The bus ride back to the visitor centre was pretty subdued. I think everyone aboard had experienced the same feeling. Although nobody said it, it seemed that we were no longer just French, German, English, Australian, American, Asian or African; nor Protestant, Catholic, Orthodox, Jewish, Muslim, or tree worshipper. We are all humans, with the same dreams, fears, hopes and weaknesses that the vanished people of Newgrange had five thousand years ago.

Back at the visitor centre, I called the B&B we had booked in Dublin for directions on how to get there. Peggie Massey gave us very specific directions and assured us that we couldn't miss it. (Warning bell!)

We headed back down the "other" road to Drogheda, joined N1 again, and before long ended up right where everyone had told us to avoid: the centre of Dublin in rush hour. Street signs in Dublin are little tiny plaques on the second story walls of buildings, impossible to read. It makes little difference, though, because the street names change every two or three blocks. Add to this that every intersection has five or six streets converging on it making a drive through the city your worst nightmare. We were surrounded on all sides by double-decker buses full of smug smiling tourists, so we couldn't do much but stick with the traffic.

We didn't do too badly for a while. I recognized landmarks: the General Post Office, the statue of Daniel O'Connell, and the bridge over the Liffey. However, when we crossed the bridge, we took a wrong turn and got completely disoriented. I pulled into an empty parking spot on the street, found a phone booth, called Peggie and told her where I thought we were. It turned out we weren't that far off. She gave me a new set of directions, and we found the place in about five minutes. Dublin isn't as big a city as I had imagined.

We lucked out on this B&B too. I had booked the place in May over the phone, because it's hard to get accommodations in Dublin in September—sports tournaments and the like. This place was in the embassy section of town, and was very quiet and safe. The house itself was a big Tudor style place with a well-kept yard and a surrounding brick wall. Peggie greeted us graciously, introduced us to Jack, the housedog, and showed us to our room. Actually the room was more like a suite. It was so nice we felt like bums messing up the place. On the entrance level to the room was a foyer with a very large bathroom off to the side, and down a few steps a bedroom with a fireplace and the biggest bed I'd ever seen. It reminded me of a line from The *Quiet Man*, "You'd have to be a sprinter to catch your wife in a bed like that!" (Whatever you're thinking right now, forget it.)

We celebrated our arrival with a very large Bushmill's. I had taken the pledge when we left Dundalk, and vowed I wouldn't touch the crayture until we were safely parked in Dublin. Now here we were, safe and unscathed. Gawd! Did that wonderful amber fluid taste good!

We rested up a bit and set out on foot to explore the neighbourhood. We knew by now that in Ireland there's always a pub nearby, and sure enough, a five-minute walk brought us to an intersection with four of them clustered together. We went into Bellamy's and surveyed the place. The young after-work business crowd, Irish yuppies, was in there relaxing after a hard day of impressing colleagues.

We left Bellamy's and crossed the street to find a place to eat. We stopped at Crowe's, where it was quieter and much less crowded. They served food here, but it looked like a cafeteria style system, so we just had a pint and went back to Bellamy's.

The crowd had thinned out some by this time, so we took a table and ordered some dinner. We split a plate of delicious fried mushrooms, and Micki had the "gourjons of plaice," a fish dish that we weren't familiar with. We found out later on that plaice is a species of flatfish similar to flounder or sole, but stronger in flavour. I ordered a burger with black pudding, but found out that they were out of the black pudding, so they substituted bacon. Burgers in Ireland aren't necessarily flat cakes of ground beef. This one was a softball-sized meatball surrounded by potatoes and other vegetables. It was quite good and filling.

We left Bellamy's and crossed the street again. Near Crowe's is Paddy Cullen's, where we ordered an after dinner Irish Mist and took it out to the sidewalk tables, where we could watch the street crowd and the full moon. Dubliners are street people and the passing show on the sidewalk was fascinating. Nearly everyone greeted us as they went by. About 5 feet away from Paddy Cullen's is Mary Mac's, so we ordered another drink there and brought it out to the same table. The property line is a little blurred, I guess.

At 11:30, we strolled home, well-fed and contented. The British Embassy is a block from Peggie's and has very tight security. The Irish police (*Gardai*) are always nearby. A rioting mob burned the place down in 1972 after Bloody Sunday in Ulster, and I guess they don't want a repeat performance. Anyway it's a good landmark.

We crashed about midnight and looked forward to a fine couple of days in Dublin's Fair City.

DUBBALIN MEN

SEPTEMBER 12. This was our first full day in Dublin. I was looking forward to it— no driving! We had a mission today: to locate (and of course visit) three of the most famous pubs in Dublin—The Stag's Head, The Brazen Head, and McDaid's. At 8:30 we went down to Peggie's very attractive dining room. It looked out the back of the house on a garden of the English variety: meticulously groomed to look completely wild and natural. The rather posh section of the city we were in reminded me of the rural Irish term for upper class Dubliners—"West Brits." Be that as it may, I thought the neighbourhood was attractive and congenial, and we were well satisfied with our accommodations.

Our choice for breakfast today for both of us was a fruit, cheese and yoghurt plate, followed by smoked salmon and scrambled eggs, accompanied by the usual warm brown bread and butter. Delicious and filling as usual.

There was a couple from Australia at breakfast with us. We were running into quite a few Australians along the way, and the reason became apparent; most of them were escaping the Olympics. Sydney was so congested and infected with Olympic fever that a lot of people were just plain escaping the nuttiness.

There was another couple with us at breakfast, young honeymooners Suzanne and Robert from Toronto. We all exchanged stories and tips about getting around in Ireland. It was a very pleasant breakfast.

We had been told that public transportation in Dublin is excellent, so that was our mode of travel for the next two days. The city buses run every ten minutes to the city centre (*An Lár* in Gaelic), and there was a bus stop right in front of our B&B. Actually, we could have easily walked downtown, as Dublin is surprisingly small in area, but we thought we'd probably be loaded down with stuff on the way back, so we opted for the bus. Bus fare is a little stiff (85p), but the convenience was worth it. We were at the foot of the O'Connell Street Bridge in less than ten minutes.

We had gotten used to the fact that nothing in Ireland is square or straight, so we had armed ourselves with a very detailed map of the heart of Dublin. It was excellent; it even marked the location of various pubs.

Walking around Dublin isn't half as scary as driving. With our security blanket map, we were really getting proud of ourselves. We went first to the city tourist centre, located in what was once St. Andrew's Church. There is a great gift shop there and information on just about anything. I wanted to find out about ferry service to Wales from Rosslare Harbour, where we would be on Friday. I obtained information about the ferries, but the government-run Tourist Board was not allowed to make any reservations. However, they did tell me how to go about doing it for myself. I really admire the Tourist Board people. They field the same dumb questions all day long and never seem to lose their cool. Micki did some shopping, and we were soon back out on the street.

It was now 11:00 and you know what that means. Indeed you do. Pubs are now open, in case you haven't been paying attention. Across the street from the Tourist Centre is O'Neill's, where we were obligated to visit for a ceremonial pint. Unwilling as we might have been, we felt that two days in Dublin should start here, since O'Neill's is the opening scene of Andrew Greeley's novel *Irish Gold*. Actually, it is a comfortably scruffy place with the nooks and crannies we've come to expect. The place was pretty empty and smelled like disinfectant; they had just finished cleaning up when we came in. In fact, I nearly tripped over a scrub bucket as I was coming down a step.

We left O'Neill's after a very satisfying full pint (within sight of the brewery, I might add), and started out for St. Patrick's Cathedral. However, since nothing is straight in Ireland, we naturally didn't go straight there. Somewhere nearby was (and has been since 1770) the Stag's Head, a definitely don't-miss establishment, and the first of our three goals. We had been told that it would be difficult to find, since it's stuck back in an alley. We simply turned a corner, and there it was. We didn't find it, we stumbled onto it.

The Stag's Head is small but very attractive. The walls and ceiling are all dark wood. There are wrought iron chandeliers hanging from the ceiling, and a large mounted deer head in the centre of the back bar. Quiet and dignified without being stuffy. I asked the barman if I could take a picture, and he told me to go ahead and take as many as I wanted to. I think he was pleased that a tourist bothered to ask.

We finished our pints and went back out on the street. Right at this moment, the essential ingredient of Irish pub-crawling hit us. The secret that has been hidden for centuries and kept from the uninitiated was suddenly revealed. The key phrase is "I gotta pee."

You see, it works like this: Every pub in Ireland has a sign stating that only customers may use the restrooms: "Toilets" as they so bluntly put it. So if you go into a pub and have a pint, and remember that a pint in the British Isles is 20 ounces, it will take about as long as it takes to get out on the street for that pint to start putting a strain on the bladder. Naturally, you can't just turn around and go back inside and head for the toilet. This would be unforgivably rude, and the Irish have been known to hold grudges against rude people for centuries. Besides, everyone in the place would be snickering because they know exactly what you're up to.

The only thing to do is to go into the next pub, order a pint and, while it's being pulled, run for the toilet. You return to the bar feeling tremendously lighter, pay for your pint, sit down and enjoy it. You get up, say goodbye to all the other patrons and go out on the street—and the process starts all over again.

Fortunately, pubs, in Dublin anyway, are seldom over 20 feet apart, so the cycle can go on indefinitely. Hence, a pub-crawl is not a depraved drunken odyssey. It's really nothing more than an extended concentrated effort to avoid wetting your pants. The secret is out at last.

Our next stop in the toilet-pint-next pub ritual was the Dame Tavern. Micki went to the facilities and while she was occupied, I had a chance to witness the feared Traffic Wardens at work. These peace officers would be called meter maids in the US, but that's way too mild a term for these ferocious Valkyries. Their duty is to see that swift and terrible punishment falls on the heads of such *amadons* (fools) that flout parking regulations. The two that I saw, and I'm assuming they were typical of their kind, were about 6 feet tall, weighed in at about 225, and were dressed in brown uniforms that would make the Gestapo envious.

From what I'd heard, Dublin never had a parking problem until recently. Relatively few people had cars, and those were small ones at that. With the new economy, nearly everyone has a car, and the recent prosperity allows for the purchase of much larger vehicles. Therefore, parking spaces are now at a premium. There are several parking ramps similar to ours, but not nearly enough. If you want to look for street parking, you can purchase a parking "disk," a small paper circle that you stick in your window that declares how much time you've paid for. If the Traffic Wardens discover an expired disk, their vengeance is swift and severe. They will call a tow truck and have your car impounded immediately; the ransom is £100. If you happen to return to your car just before they call a tow truck, you can pay your fine on the spot and get away, no doubt with a lecture on trying to flout the law.

The two wardens that I watched out the pub window apparently had come across a car with a disk about to expire. The pub patrons inside were also watching, with little mutters about getting rid of one set of tyrants and installing another. The owner of the car came up in the nick of time, talked to the wardens for a minute and then drove away. I guess this time the innocent and downtrodden won out over the oppressive government.

We walked down Dame Street, which becomes Lord Edward Street, and turned left onto Werburgh Street. The cycle was kicking in again, so we stopped in at the Castle Inn Pub. We did the toilet/pint ritual there and headed back down Werburgh Street, which has now changed its name to Bridge Street. A right turn onto Bull Alley Street brought us to the formal garden adjacent to St. Patrick's Cathedral.

Jonathan Swift, the author of Gulliver's *Travels* and a satirist who blasted the English government of his day with a tongue like a yard of vinegar, but had a generous and compassionate heart for the Irish people, was dean of St. Patrick's in the early eighteenth century and is buried inside the cathedral. Part of Swift's estate endowed the establishment of a mental hospital in Dublin. With a last bit of sarcasm, Swift supposedly stated that no country deserved or needed it more.

St. Patrick's is beautiful in an old English sort of way. It is majestic and dignified, not Celtic at all. The cathedral also has the honour of being the site of the first performance of Handel's *Messiah*, now sung every Christmas in the cathedral. That would certainly be a spectacle worth attending.

Handel's other claim to fame (and to my mind, just as important) was his discovery of O'Carolan and his music. According to the story, Handel just happened to hear an old blind harper playing on the street. He was intrigued by what he heard and persuaded the harper to play for him so that he could transcribe the melodies. So because of Handel's interest, the world now knows Turlough O'Carolan and the music of the last great Gaelic harper.

After coming out of St. Patrick's, we needed relief from all that majesty. We also felt the cycle kicking in again. Across the street from the cathedral is a little workingman's pub—Nash's. This is the type of place that you can well imagine revolution at work 85 years ago. I would guess that the decor hasn't changed since then either. There are pictures of Collins, Pearse, Connelly and the others all over the walls. There is one especially spooky old photograph of the rebels in 1916 heading to their doom at the GPO.

There was an older fellow sitting across the room from us with a pint in front of him, who kept nodding off to sleep. If his hair had been white, he could have been a spitting image of my grandfather Dan Welsh. I had 800-speed film in my camera and no need for flash, so I sneaked a surreptitious shot of him. It came out perfect.

We were collecting advertising lighters along the way for souvenirs, so we asked the barman if they had any with Nash's name on them. He said they did, but they were in the cellar and "Why do you want one anyway?" We told him we were collecting them from all the memorable places we'd been. That seemed to be the right answer, so he pulled up the trap door and went downstairs and brought us up a few.

We left Nash's and headed back toward the Liffey. That river is a great landmark for keeping your bearings. We weren't too far up the street when Nash's refreshments kicked in again. (Dear Lord, make me lose interest in Guinness before my kidneys crump; say at about age 120.) We stopped in at Darkey Kelley's, where the ambience is Dublin literary. The place has a reading-room atmosphere with little snugs lined with books. I liked the place.

After we had performed the ritual, we headed out on the street for a short walk to Christchurch Cathedral. This is another Anglican High Church establishment. (Catholic Lite—all the incense, none of the guilt.) It was quite impressive—very medieval. We paid our respects at the tomb of Richard De Clare, Earl of Pembroke, who led the first Norman invasion of Ireland, and ended up more Irish than the natives. More about him later.

We were only a few blocks from the second of our stated goals: the Brazen Head, the oldest pub in Ireland. We found it without much difficulty on Bridge Street Lower. It is claimed that it has been a pub since 1198, but was licensed by Charles II in 1666. Patriots Theobald Wolfe-Tone and Robert Emmet were regulars here in the early 1800's.

The Brazen Head gets its name from an old story concerning one of the many rebellions against English rule in Ireland. A battle was going on in the street outside the pub, and an overly curious red haired woman stuck her head out the window to see the action. An errant sword stroke by one of the soldiers promptly decapitated her. The pub was renamed in remembrance of this unfortunate incident.

Since it was 4:00 PM now, we had a lunch/supper here. The place does look 800 years old, so we just sat and soaked up the atmosphere and a pint while waiting for our order. Micki had an Irish stew and I had the Dublin Coddle. Now this last is supposed to be the essential Dublin comfort food. Even James Joyce, who wasn't respectful about much of anything, wrote respectfully about Dublin Coddle. The sight of it alone though would give a buzzard nausea. It's a sort of scalloped potato dish with large pieces of carrot and onion, and big chunks of bacon and sausage. In spite of its looks, it was very tasty. It contained the two essential ingredients of Irish home cooking: potatoes and cured pork.

Fairly well stuffed, we walked back to the city centre on the south bank of the Liffey, heading for the General Post Office. It was not a far walk to the O'Connell Street Bridge, where we took a left, crossed the bridge and walked the two blocks to the Post Office. Looking at the building from across O'Connell Street, it was pretty easy to imagine the doings of Easter Monday 1916. However, the tour buses all over the place rather distracted from the mood.

Earl Street North runs east off O'Connell opposite the General Post Office. A short block down Earl is Madigan's Pub, one of James Joyce's favourite hangouts. We stepped in and found a quiet table to have a pint. It's a large well-maintained Edwardian sort of place. It's not a kids' place, so it just suited us—nice and quiet and subdued.

I could well imagine Joyce frequenting this place. He was a dignified man and rather reserved. He outraged much of the Irish population of his time with his strange style of prose, and offended the very religious with his unsubtle sexual references. Still, even though he spent much of his life abroad, he considered Dublin his home, and it provided him with a rich texture of characters and settings.

A couple of blocks east of Madigan's on what has now become Talbot Street is a rather upscale shopping area. We stopped in at Eason's Books and bought a few things, Maeve Binchy's latest novel, and some CD's and tapes. Practically next door is The Celt. This is a very small cozy pub with a pharmacy motif. Apparently it really was once a pharmacy because there are antique shelves with little boxes and bottles all over the walls. As we were having our pint, the owner came over and gave us a kindly lecture on being very careful about theft. I had put my camera on a chair next to me, and he felt it was his duty to inform innocent Americans of the dangers they could encounter. Theft in Dublin was rampant, he said, but "It won't happen in here." We thanked him for his concern and he went away satisfied he'd done at least one work of mercy for the day.

Wandering back toward the Liffey, we stopped at Sean O'Casey's, a sort of working class pub. While we were enjoying our pint, I got to wondering how we were going to find McDaid's. The very helpful barman got us a map and showed us how to get there. McDaid's is over on the south side of the Liffey, approximately 10 blocks away. We finished up, thanked him and headed back across the O'Connell Street Bridge.

We had to visit McDaid's because of Brendan Behan, one of my favourite Irish characters. He was at various times in his short life, a notorious juvenile delinquent, IRA activist, explosives expert, Gaelic poet, journalist, playwright, lyricist, popular television talk show guest, prodigious drinker, and general pain-in-the-arse to whatever government in whose jurisdiction he happened to be.

He came from a rebellious, socialist, working class but highly literate family and became involved in IRA activity at the age of ten. He learned the art of explosives in his early teens from *Na Fianna*, the IRA youth group. From age sixteen to twenty-two, he spent most of his time in prison for various IRA actions. During this time, he honed his skills in the most deadly of Irish weapons: the power of the written word. His sardonic yet lyrical *Borstal Boy*, a modern classic, is his reminiscence of this time.

His play *The Quare Fellow* and the raw harsh lyrics of "The Old Triangle" recall his years in an Irish prison, convicted for attempted murder in a botched IRA rescue. The ironic disillusionment of "The Patriot Game", a standard with most Irish musicians, reflects on the life of a rebel and its ultimate tragic end.

Amnestied from prison in 1943, Brendan became less of a criminal and more of a caustic social commentator. He also became more of a celebrity, and took up some of the less desirable traits that accompany sudden fame. Stories told about him are still legends in Dublin pubs.

One that stands out concerns the time he was deported from England and sent back to Ireland. As he was going through immigration, the harried officer on duty asked him the first question on the official list without looking up from his stack of papers: "Nationality?" Without hesitation, Brendan replied, "Yemeni Arab." Still without looking up, the official answered, "Welcome back to Ireland, Brendan."

With his drinking out of control and his diabetes worsening, Brendan's health deteriorated at the same rate that his popularity increased. In March 1964, he collapsed and died. He was forty-one.

McDaid's, Brendan Behan's favourite hangout, is up a little alley off Graffton Street. Brendan is supposed to have been kicked out of 720 pubs in Dublin alone, but McDaid's probably tolerated him because the place itself is the stuff of legends. One story concerns a time when the pub was in financial difficulties and was in imminent danger of closing for good. On the last day before McDaid's was to close, a patron walked in and looked at the scruffy motley collection of would-be poets, novelists, and playwrights strewn about in various stages of deep inebriation, who would have no place to go when the pub closed. The man observed, "The sinking ship is deserting its rats." McDaid's was saved at the last minute and remains a hangout for aspiring writers.

The pub is a rather small place, and it was fairly crowded, but there was an empty table out on the sidewalk. I ordered a couple of pints to take outside. It was a pleasant evening, and watching people on the street in Dublin is always fascinating. I gave Brendan a silent toast and hummed "The Patriot Game." Nobody in the vicinity thought it was peculiar. Not at McDaid's.

We were winding down now, so we headed back across the Liffey for just one more. We crossed over on the Halfpenny Bridge and stopped at the Arlington Hotel on Bachelor's Walk, a street that runs right alongside the river. The hotel bar is large and pretty noisy, with little character.

We finished up and went back out on the street to catch our bus home. There was a bus stop right next to the O'Connell Street Bridge so we figured that was where we caught our bus. There wasn't any bus with our route number on it, so a nice old guy saw our problem and told us we could catch our bus at the stop on the other side of the river. We went back across the Liffey one more time to the south side and found the right bus. Don't tell me I don't know the O'Connell Street Bridge. We had crossed it four times today.

It wasn't all that late, but we crashed early. It had been a pretty full day, getting acquainted with the city streets, accompanied by the genial ghosts of James Joyce and Brendan Behan, the quintessential "Dubbalin" Men.

THE TART WITH THE CART

SEPTEMBER 13. Today marked the halfway point of the trip. This was our second full day in Dublin, and we were getting to feel very cosmopolitan. We didn't get lost yesterday; we visited twelve pubs, two cathedrals, and observed several monuments. Today would be the day to just drift in the city and go wherever the momentary whim took us.

We were alone at breakfast this morning, since all the other guests had already left the house or the city. Peggie's arrangement was for us to fix our own toast in a toaster on the sideboard while our breakfasts were being prepared. However, the toaster wasn't working so we opted for the brown bread and butter instead. The malfunctioning toaster sent Peggie into a minor tizzy. She didn't want to mess with the electricity for fear of knocking the whole house out and herself with hungry guests (the two of us) entirely. By the time she'd figured out a solution, we'd each had a couple of big slices of brown bread. Peggie decided that she would make toast for us in the kitchen and bring it out to us. By the time we got to the Full Irish Breakfast, we'd each eaten about a loaf and a half of bread. Much walking was in order for the day to get shed of breakfast.

Before we left for the city centre, I called Stena Ferry Lines about ferry passage from Rosslare Harbour to Fishguard, Wales. Having no experience in booking ferry reservations, I felt a little ignorant, but the agent at the other end was extremely helpful. There was daily service from Rosslare with departure at 8:30 AM and return at 4:00 PM. Foot passenger tickets were only £17 per person (round trip), just half of what I'd thought they'd be. The guy told me he could make a reservation on the phone and our tickets would be waiting at the port. I asked him if he needed a deposit of some sort, but he said it wasn't necessary. He was very pleasant and ended our conversation with "Thank you for your patronage, Mr. Lovelace, and God bless you, sir!" Those folks could teach Americans a few things about customer service.

At 10:00 we caught the bus for the city centre. We were getting to be such old hands at this that we even had the correct change ready. Today's mission was shopping—souvenirs, gifts and an Irish Harley shirt for George, one of Micki's colleagues. The Harley Davidson store was easy to find (in fact, there are two of them within several blocks of each other). We were more or less confining ourselves today to the Trinity College-Graffton Street-Temple Bar area. This is where the Dublin street life is at its best: interesting shops, trendy cafes, and no shortage of pubs.

The pulse of Dublin beats on Graffton Street, a pedestrian-only stretch of about four blocks. The variety of shops, cafes, and pubs runs the gamut from centuries old to the brand new and tacky. Bewley's Oriental Cafe, a Dublin institution known for its fine teas, coffee and pastries, is a half block away from Burger King. Since there are no cars, the street is full of musicians, street vendors, and panhandlers. There's a constant tide of businessmen and women, loafers, hawkers, and tourists flowing around the street. We checked out a few gift shops and examined a street stand selling exquisite Celtic silverwork where I bought a silver Celtic cross with a jade inlay for my good friend and co-worker Bernette. I think I was cheated £5 in the transaction, but I guess that's the admission fee for the daylong circus on Graffton.

Dubliners are proud of their history and the city has numerous monuments dedicated to people, ideals, and important events. In spite of their respect for these monuments, Dubliners' respect is tempered by a strong dose of good-natured Irish irreverence, to prevent anyone or anything from becoming too pompous or self-important. Most monuments have been tagged with some witty nickname.

A case in point is the statue of Molly Malone, the fishmonger heroine of Dublin's most famous song. A dramatic bronze sculpture of Molly and her wheelbarrow stands on a corner of the Graffton and Nassau Streets intersection. This version of Molly doesn't seem to be dying of the fever. She is a curvaceous full-figured young woman whose dress is cut to show a great deal of delightful cleavage. When the statue was put into place, there was a good deal of comment on the seemliness of poor Molly's attire. Nonetheless, Molly's dress remained unmodified, and the statue has been dubbed "The Tart with the Cart."

Of course, being in the neighbourhood, we couldn't pass up the opportunity to photograph Molly. However, the base of the statue provides the denizens of Graffton an excellent seat for eating lunch, reading the paper, or waiting for the bus. There was no way we could get a decent picture of her by herself, so we had to content ourselves with a postcard instead.

As we walked past Fitzsimon's Hotel and Pub on Wellington Quay, a short distance from Graffton, we noticed a sign advertising traditional music in the evening. We mentally noted that this might be our evening's entertainment.

"Quay" is pronounced "key" or "kay" and designates a riverbank or port. All the streets fronting the Liffey are quays of one name or another: Wellington Quay, Ormond Quay, Aston Quay, etc. We strolled along the south side of the Liffey for several blocks and stopped opposite the Four Courts on the north side of the river. We were standing on the spot where the Free Staters pounded the building with artillery during the Irish Civil War. It made me shiver.

At 11:00 sharp, amazingly enough, we found ourselves at the Daniel O'Connell Pub. You will discern along the way that Daniel O'Connell is a very popular figure in Irish history, and in fact has become a major figure in Irish folklore. He was Lord Mayor of Dublin in the 1840's, and was called the Great Liberator. Every other pub in Ireland seems to claim that O'Connell hung out in their establishment. If that were even half-true, he'd have had to spend about 40 hours a day in pubs, with no time left for liberating. At any rate, this pub claimed that he spent a lot of time on the premises. It was a nice little place to have your first pint of the day.

We had a minor disaster here. As I was about to take a sip of Guinness, the left lens of my glasses fell out of its frame onto the bar. We had no way of fixing it, but fortunately there was a pharmacy right next door. We finished our pints and went next door to purchase a repair kit. I hadn't lost the tiny screw that secures the lens in the frame, so we managed to get it repaired in short order, but the idea of spending the next week and a half without glasses was pretty frightening.

Properly refreshed and repaired, we headed for Trinity College to see the Book of Kells. By now, avoiding guided tours has become a point of honour. We found that just walking around on our own was much more flexible and satisfying.

Queen Elizabeth I founded Trinity College in 1592 as a fortress against Popery and it looks like a European university is supposed to look— old dignified buildings and young undignified students. Making our way across the campus to the library, we heard a few tour groups getting their lectures from student guides. It sounded to me like political speeches more than historical information. I don't think the tour guides realized that forty or so blue-haired old American ladies didn't have the foggiest idea what they were being told.

The Book of Kells is a gospel book hand lettered sometime in the seventh or eighth century when Irish Celtic Christianity was in its golden age. How the book survived the centuries must be some sort of miracle. The book is kept in a glass case in a room where the light, temperature and humidity are very strictly controlled. Each day, a different page is displayed. I had pictured the book in my mind as much bigger in size than it actually is—it is only about 8 by 10 inches. The subdued light made it a little difficult to see all the details clearly, but it was impressive nonetheless. Actually, I learned more about it from the excellent interpretive gallery adjacent to the room where the book is kept. There are very clear and detailed explanations about Irish monasticism, calligraphy, Celtic symbolism and medieval Ireland.

The next goal was Magill's Delicatessen in a little side street off Graffton. The place is tiny, but stacked to the ceiling with all sorts of wonderful smelling delicacies—smoked salmon, hams, cheeses, and a big variety of jams and jellies. I took Micki's picture in the doorway, one of the few times we acted touristy. We bought an assortment of jams to take home, and also a fist sized hunk of a farmhouse cheese made in Doolin. We walked down the street nibbling that cheese for lunch. It was very tasty, and made us homesick for Doolin and the wild West Clare coast as opposed to the big impersonal city, etc., etc. Eating cheese and thinking sentimental Irish thoughts can sometimes make you melancholy.

There's only one cure for sloppy Irish sentimentality: a pint of Guinness to comfort the soul. Fortunately, there was a pub within five paces—The Duke, Michael Collins' favourite pub.

Collins was one of the few practical, realistic players in the Irish revolution of 1916. A banker by profession, he realized more than the other older but more romantic rebels that building a nation would be an extremely long and delicate process. He realized better than his comrades that permanent freedom required negotiation and compromise, as well as courage and willingness to die.

Along with Padraic Pearse, Eamon De Valera, Sean MacBride, Thomas MacDonagh and the others, Collins was arrested at the surrender of the rebel-occupied General Post Office in late April 1916. Unlike the other leaders, perhaps because of his age (26), he was not executed but interned by the British government and released in December.

Collins was named commander of the rebel forces during the Anglo-Irish War of 1917–21. With few resources except brains and grit, he engineered a deadly campaign of terror against the British. With a carefully developed spy system within the government, Collins could anticipate when and where the British army would be most vulnerable. Collins' force of urban guerrillas would strike a police station or army post with devastating effect and then swiftly vanish into the countryside or the maze of Dublin's alleys.

After a few years of embarrassing stalemate and the pressure of world opinion, the British government suggested a truce and treaty discussions. Collins was well aware that a small ill-equipped rebel army could not battle the British Empire forever and urged the provisional Irish parliament to discuss terms with the British. Collins reluctantly agreed to be part of the treaty negotiations in London.

After several months of weary negotiation, the delegation returned to Dublin with a treaty. It wasn't perfect—it designated the three southern provinces of Ireland as the Irish Free State with its own parliament, but kept Ulster as a province of Great Britain—but the delegation felt that it was the best the Irish could get.

The Irish parliament voted for the acceptance of the treaty by an extremely narrow margin, but the dissenters, led by Eamon DeValera, refused to recognize the treaty and walked out of the session.

What followed was the terrible tragedy of the Irish Civil War, pitting Free Staters against the anti-treaty forces, former comrades but now deadly enemies. Collins sadly assumed command of the Free State forces and achieved a few victories, particularly the shelling of the Four Courts from across the Liffey, but the war dragged on inconclusively, mainly because the skills he had taught his former friends were now being used against the Free State.

In the fall of 1922, in rural County Cork, a small convoy of vehicles led by Collins was ambushed. During a brief exchange of gunfire, Michael Collins was killed by a rifle bullet to the head. He was only 31 years old.

The Free State and the IRA in time stopped the bloody waste of the civil war. DeValera eventually became prime minister and served his country well for the rest of his very long life, but the bitter division about the government of Ulster persists to this day.

The Duke is a nice inconspicuous little old place with few pretensions. I can well imagine Michael Collins using it for a headquarters. After we had entered, Micki sat down at a table and I went up to the bar to order. As our pints were being pulled, a rather hefty guy came up to where I was standing. He had gone to the toilet, and I had inadvertently taken his spot. I apologized, and he said, "No problem at all. Just give me enough room to get me fat arse in there." As I said, few pretensions.

We were in an area of the city known as Temple Bar, the traditional lair of poets, novelists, actors, politicians, newspaper reporters, and a hundred varieties of wannabees. The pubs are even closer together here, if you can imagine, than other parts of the city. We made a stop at the Palace Bar, another little old place, where a number of people were reading or doing crossword puzzles. Here at the Palace, while we were resting with our load of loot, I came up with the idea of taking our goodies back to Peggie's and returning to the city centre later unburdened for the night's entertainment.

Micki concurred, but there were a few more shops she wanted to visit. On the way to Blarney Woollen Mills on Nassau Street, we made a quick detour into Oliver St. John Gogarty's (named after one of James Joyce's friends), supposedly the heart of traditional music in Dublin. It was another old-fashioned bar, dark wood, crooked corners and the rest. We had our pints and headed for the Auld Dubliner across the street. This place too advertised traditional music in the evening, so we put this place on the list of the evening's possibilities.

We walked back up Fleet Street, around the Trinity College wall and down Nassau to Blarney Woollen Mills. I wasn't too interested in looking at yarn, so I went a few doors down the street to the Lord Kildare to sit while Micki shopped. We had gotten so confident that we actually split up and went our own ways for a bit.

The Lord Kildare was just cleaning up their luncheon buffet, and there was nobody at the bar. I waited until a young fellow came up behind the bar, asked him for a pint, and he served me. As I was sitting there, four women came in and I got to chatting with them. I'll give you the details later, but suffice it to say that I wished at that point I wouldn't be identified as American, their behaviour was so boorish.

Micki came in and rescued me and we headed back to the bus stop, rode back to Peggie's and dumped our load. We rested for a little over an hour and started out to sample Dublin nightlife.

As we were leaving the house, a couple had just come up to the door. They thought we were the proprietors, and started asking us about a room. We referred them to Peggie and went on our way.

It was 5:00 now so we hopped the bus again and headed for Temple Bar. We could see a lot of little interesting pubs along the way, but there was no way that we could get at them. Too bad—so much Guinness, so little time.

Temple Bar has no shortage of pubs. We stepped into Bowe's, a cozy little place, which has marvellous polished brass tabletops. We had just a half-pint here, since the night was young.

When we got back out on the street, there was a gentle misty rain falling, what the Irish call a fine soft evening. The pavement was wet enough to reflect the shine of streetlights, and people were cheerfully ambling about under umbrellas. The scene was so movie-like that it was a little hard to keep a grip on reality. The Oliver St. John Gogarty was only a half block away, and we could hear fiddle and pennywhistle music floating down the street.

The place was crowded, but we managed to get our pints and nudged our way closer to the musicians. They were young folks and very good. You could imagine that this session had been a nightly ritual for the last hundred years.

There is a restaurant over the bar, and since it was now 6 o'clock, we went upstairs for dinner. Seating for dinner in Irish restaurants is a little different from here. We were taken to a table for six already occupied by an elderly couple. Americans have a much more acute sense of privacy than the Irish apparently do. We don't usually sit down with people we don't know, but it seems that the Irish think nothing of sitting down to dinner with total strangers. We asked to be seated at another table, telling the hostess that we would like a window view. She took us to another table for six that was unoccupied. Actually there wasn't a table for only two in the whole place.

We were soon joined by an older fellow (actually about my age) that Micki thought was mentally challenged. I thought he was probably a professor at Trinity. I think we were both right. He was a nice fellow who kept to himself, and didn't intrude into our conversation. A nice-looking young couple also joined us. So our dinner for two turned out to be dinner for five.

The young couple ordered a "starter" (Irish term for appetizer) of a pot of mussels. The waitress brought this big cooking pot full of mussels and plunked it on the table and they dove into it. The pot looked to be about a gallon in capacity, and was full up to the top with mussels in a delicious smelling broth. I had all I could do to keep from belting out a few choruses of "Molly Malone," but I restrained myself.

Our food arrived and we dug in. Micki had what was termed Arthur's Casserole, supposed to be a beef stew with Guinness. Actually, it was a sort of vegetable beef soup. I had the cabbage and bacon. Bacon in Ireland can be any cut of cured and smoked pork, so what I got was something like ham and cabbage. It was satisfying, but not outstanding.

While we were eating, a group of Americans was seated at an adjacent table. I'll get into the details of this later, but "Ugly American" certainly came to mind.

We went back downstairs to the bar where the music was still going on. It was also still crowded, so we left. We stopped in at The Quay, which seemed to be a sort of college student hangout. It was pretty noisy for an Irish pub. Normally, pubs, even when crowded, are fairly quiet. We had a quick half-pint and went on our way.

We were more or less aiming for Fitzsimon's where the music was supposed to be exceptional. On the way, we stopped at the Ha'Penny Bridge Inn, on Aston Quay on the Liffey. The Ha'Penny Bridge is right in front of the pub. The bridge is named for the fact that it once was a toll bridge for foot traffic, and the toll was 1/2 penny. Now the bridge is just a curiosity and a tourist attraction.

It was a lot quieter in this pub. There was an older barman who flattered Micki no end by calling her "lady" and "sweetheart." There's no doubt that the Irish honed the gift of gab into an art form. It was quiet when we entered, but a few of the patrons wanted to watch soccer on TV, and the noise level went up a few notches, so we left and headed for Fitzsimon's.

Fitzsimon's has a fairly large bar area with a stage built up in the corner for the musicians. It was pretty crowded when we got there, but there were two stools open at the bar. We made a beeline for them and settled in. We had a good view of the stage, and the bartender was a good-natured young fellow who assured us we had the best seats in the house.

To settle the huge meal we just had, I ordered a double Jameson's. Micki was concerned that I would drink the bus fare home, but the bartender assured us that he wouldn't let that happen. He said that he hears that every night.

While we were watching the crowd, we got into a conversation with a young Aussie. He of course asked us where we were from, and when we told him we were from Minnesota, he told us he had once gone with a girl from St. Paul, but broke up with her because she was too religious. We asked him what he was doing in Dublin, and he gave us the expected answer: he was escaping the Olympics. He then went into an indignant (and very funny) tirade in a perfect Crocodile Dundee accent about the insanity in Sydney: "All ya see for the past two months on TV is some little half naked guy runnin' down the road with a torch stuck in the air! Who needs it? Nobody in Sydney can afford tickets to the games, the traffic is a nightmare, and besides, who gives a rat's ass anyway?"

That pretty well summed it up, and he wished us a pleasant holiday and drifted away. It was still some time before the music started, so we started watching the show behind the bar. A little skinny kid had started working behind the bar, and I'd swear he was James Joyce's great grandson: thin face, thick glasses and a frail physique. He was yakky and a bit snappy and thoroughly entertaining. A southern American woman came up to the bar and in a very pronounced drawl ordered a "pahnt of Guinness and a pahnt of cidah." Without a blink, the kid repeated her order in the exact same accent that he'd heard it in, adding "Will that be it for y'all?" It went clean over her head.

The entertainment soon started and was excellent. Four musicians played the old tunes and periodically four teenaged girls step danced. They were very skilled, and the stage reverberated with that pounding rhythm reminiscent of Riverdance. I enjoyed it immensely.

The last bus runs at 11:30, so we headed down the street a few short blocks to catch it. (No, I didn't drink the bus fare.) As we were boarding the bus, the couple we had met at Peggie's door joined us. Being the old Dubliners that we now were, we offered to guide them home. Ten minutes later we were at Peggie's and two minutes after that, we were sound asleep, resting after a strenuous but very delightful day.

FOLLOW ME TO CARLOW

SEPTEMBER 14. At 8:30 AM we went down to another of Peggie's incredible breakfasts. Robert and Suzanne, the Canadian honeymooners, were already seated. Today they planned to go to the airport and pick up a car to try their driving skills. They wanted to see the Giants' Causeway and the Cliffs of Moher. They didn't seem to have a clue as to where these places were, and couldn't care less. Ah, to be young again and not obsessed with details.

As we were chatting, the couple that rode the bus with us last night came in. They were from Scotland and were big Bob Dylan fans. Dylan was apparently in Dublin for a series of concerts this week. They told us about trying to get tickets last night to no avail, but they did manage to get ahold of some for this evening.

After breakfast, we packed up and settled up with Peggie, and said our goodbyes to both her and Jack, who manages, like most dogs, to put on a pathetic "poor old me" demeanour whenever somebody looks at him. Peggie gave us excellent directions on getting out of town and heading south, so we were on our way.

We had heard highly enthusiastic praise for Johnnie Fox's Pub, reputed to be the highest pub in Ireland. It is located in the village of Glencullen in the mountains just outside of Dublin. Frommer recommended it highly, and there's a picture of it in nearly every coffee table book on Irish scenery. It's not far from Dublin, as the city buses run there regularly. We had it in mind to have lunch there because the seafood is reputed to be excellent.

Without any difficulty, we found N11, the main road south out of Dublin; this is a dual carriageway, so we were making fine progress. We had a map that showed Glencullen, but it didn't show how to get there. We pulled off the highway at Kilmacanogue and asked for directions at a petrol station. The girl behind the counter said we'd have to ask Eamon, who was out by the pumps. It seems that guys named Eamon are sources of information. There were only about ten guys out there by the pumps, and I figured that at least eight of them were named Eamon. I asked the closest one how to get to Johnnie Fox's.

He said that we'd have to go back toward Dublin about three miles and then turn left to the town of Enniskerry, and from there on there were plenty of signs to follow. He didn't say I couldn't miss it, for which I was grateful.

We found Enniskerry without any trouble, and Eamon was right: there were plenty of signs pointing the way to Johnnie Fox's. However, the road was a regional road through the Wicklow Mountains, and it was scary even by Irish standards—narrow corners, hairpin curves, rock walls looming on the road edges. I thought I saw a couple of goats hyperventilating with fear. Maybe it was my imagination.

We didn't get lost though. Eventually we pulled up in front of Fox's. I will try, but it is impossible to describe it. The pub has been in continuous operation for 250 years, and (Surprise!) was one of Daniel O'Connell's favourite watering holes. Actually, he did live in Glencullen for a time.

The front yard is full of offbeat types of antiques—old wagons, cream separators, churns, you name it. There is also an old car from the thirties painted bright green with a license plate proclaiming FU2, which pretty well summarizes the cheerful in-your-face attitude of the place.

It was just 11:00, so we went inside and got a couple of pints to take out to a table in the front. The view was gorgeous. Glencullen sits on the top of a ridge and looks over a golf course and a long green valley to the south. It was a day of shifting clouds, so the light changed constantly. It was very pleasant to just sit and soak in the scenery.

Johnnie Fox's is a very popular place, so we wished to have an early lunch to avoid the crowd. The interior is even more incredible than the outside. There is absolutely no theme to the place except possibly "Old and Odd." There are dining rooms around corners and up small steps. There is no way of telling exactly how big the place is, because there seems to be another room leading off every other room.

Tables and chairs are made from every type of thing imaginable: old foot-treadle sewing machines, cream cans with wooden tops, and old farm implements. There is a chair carved in the shape of a human hand out of a massive block of wood. One table is made out of an old bed frame complete with head and footboard. The walls are covered with old pictures, tools, weapons, and various kinds of lamps. Even if you didn't want anything to eat or drink, just wandering around in there would be fascinating.

The lunch crowd hadn't yet arrived, and we were shown to a table in one of the little side rooms with a view out onto a slightly bigger area. The waitress was a pleasant little gal who brought us our pints and menus, and gave us a few minutes to soak up the atmosphere and decide on our lunch.

We'd been told that the seafood here was outstanding and the portions were huge, so we ordered a seafood sampler to share. This turned out to be a cold plate with every type of ocean critter imaginable on it: lobster, crab, oysters, cockles, mussels and a few other boneless things I couldn't identify. They weren't alive, alive O, but they certainly had been not too long ago. The waitress offered to take our picture with this feast, and we gladly let her. Apparently this is a customary ritual here.

We finished our lunch, settled up and wandered around the place for a bit. Quite a few celebrities have visited Fox's, and they keep a list of who's been there. Micki took a few pictures of all the little oddities around the place, including the identification on the toilet doors: two old enamelled hospital urinal basins, one male and one female. Now we were ready to leave.

We were in a fairly euphoric mood after that tremendous meal, and didn't have too far to go to Carlow, our destination for the evening. All we had to do was find N7, which eventually joins N9, which leads directly to Carlow. N7 was somewhere to the west of Glencullen.

We still had our vague map, so we headed back to Enniskerry down the frightening little road, got back on N11and headed back toward Dublin. We figured that somewhere we could turn left and easily pick up the road we wanted.

We turned to the west at a village called Stillorgan, and things began to deteriorate. We found ourselves on a regional road that curved around so much that we completely lost any sense of direction. Occasionally we could see Dublin Bay or the city itself. Sometimes we went through an area of what looked like affordable housing projects, followed by sheep pastures. We went through a construction zone that I guessed was the Dublin ring road. We kept ploughing on for what seemed like an hour through mountains and valleys. At this point we desperately needed some orientation. From our map we could see that if we discovered N81, we would be in good shape.

We came around a curve to a tee road, with a pub right on the intersection. We wheeled into The Blue Gardenia to ventilate, stretch, calm down and get directions. We managed all of it. There was a red haired freckled kid behind the bar who was very nice but seemed puzzled that we were having a problem. While we sipped our cider, he told us that N81 was right outside the door. We were in the village of Brittas, and all we had to do to get to N9 was to follow N81 a few miles to Blessington, turn right on R410 to Naas, and when we got there we would be on N7, which we would follow to Newbridge, where we would find N9, which goes directly to Carlow.

Actually, that was just a translation into American terms. What he really said was to take this road out front to Blessington and then take the Naas road and then take the Newbridge road and then the Carlow road. It all seemed pretty simple to him. Most Irish never use road numbers in giving directions. In fact, I don't think that very many of them even know what they are. They don't seem to think it's necessary.

It was pretty simple after that. Our mood had been restored, because we realized once again that we weren't as lost as we thought we were. Sure enough, the kid's directions were right on the money, and we found the correct roads. There is an old rebel song "Follow Me to Carlow," which probably wouldn't have been good advice for anyone behind us today.

About ten miles outside of Carlow is the village of Moon, where a very ancient high cross is located. We pulled off and stopped at the Moon High Cross Inn, a very old little tavern. A stretch and a half-pint and some directions were in order. The High Cross Inn has been around for a couple of centuries and used to be a stage coach stop. There are several little bar areas, without a square corner, level floor or straight wall in the place. We were told that Clint Eastwood likes to hang around in here, but I guess he wasn't in the neighbourhood. If he had been, that would have made our day.

We got our directions from the lady munching on a sandwich behind the bar. The cross was about two miles away and we found it without too much trouble. The cross was erected in the ninth century and is inside the ruins of an old church, which was apparently built around it later. There is very little to indicate that this is a tourist attraction; it's simply there in a little patch of woods overgrown by weeds and blackberry bushes. I don't know whether this was intentional, but I definitely liked it that way. It looked a lot more ancient than if the place were well groomed with plastic signs around. It was very quiet and hushed.

This definitely was another thin place, although from a different era. While the rest of Europe was being convulsed by the last centuries of the Dark Ages, this cross was carved and put into place as a monument to Celtic culture and faith. Twelve centuries later, it is still there, and we were standing at its foot.

After exploring around for awhile and taking a few pictures, we got back onto the highway and headed for Carlow. We had decided on Carlow for the night because it was about half way to Wexford and because the Browne's Hill Dolmen, a Stone Age monument, was located there. We had booked a room at T&G's Bed and Breakfast, the initials for Tom & Gerry. We got onto the Carlow roundabout and headed for the town centre. A couple of blocks in, we spotted a petrol station on the right where we could phone for directions. This is one of the few times that driving on the left caused a problem. I made the right turn across the oncoming lane, but I unconsciously pulled into the <u>right</u> lane of the driveway. There was a car coming out of the station, and of course I was in his lane. Fortunately, neither of us was going very fast, so we easily avoided each other. I tried to wave an apology, and he gave me a sort of half-amused, half-annoyed look, and we got on with it. I thought the incident would probably have caused a shootout in the US.

I called T&G's and found out we had practically just driven past the place. We had passed a cemetery on the way into town, and the B&B was just on the other side of it. So we backtracked a few blocks, went around the cemetery and found it.

The place was a rather new but fairly small house on a sort of cul-de-sac in a very clean quiet neighbourhood. A guy came out and greeted us and introduced himself as Tommy. I thought he said Tony, but I guess it was just his accent. He was pretty gabby, but very friendly and hospitable, and asked us if we would like some tea or coffee. We had been offered refreshments before at other places, and had usually passed on it, but we'd learned that the rules of Irish courtesy almost demand that you accept a gracious offer. It's considered a minor breach of etiquette to refuse.

He served us tea and scones in the sitting room and inquired how we were enjoying our trip thus far. Of course, we said we were having a great time. He wanted to know if Ireland was all that we had expected. We told him it certainly was and then some. He said he was happy to hear that because so many Americans seem to be disappointed that Ireland is so modern. He got a little annoyed (not at us) and said, "So many of them expect us to run around in little green shorts and pixie hats!"

He told us he knew we were Americans when I called him from the petrol station. (As if the accent weren't enough.) I had told him I thought we were about a half-mile southeast of the roundabout. He said Irish never talk about east and west in directions, because "Look at a map. Nothing runs straight in this country." I thought that that was the understatement of the century. I might have added that nothing is strictly right or left either.

The conversation drifted around to the truckers' protest. We had been hearing all week that the truck drivers all over Ireland (hauliers, as they're called locally) were going to stage a nationwide protest on Friday over the high price of fuel. They planned to form convoys and drive very slowly up and down major highways. Part of the plan was to circle continuously in roundabouts to slow up traffic. Tommy works in Dublin and decided he wasn't going in to work tomorrow because traffic would be unbearable. (I suspected that he was delighted at the prospect of a day off with an ironclad excuse.) Part of the protesters' plan was to snarl up traffic in major cities and towns and to partially barricade ports.

This is where it got personal—we were heading to Rosslare Harbour tomorrow, and that is a major port. I was wondering whether we were going to be able to get there or not. Tommy didn't know, but it didn't look too good. Well, it wasn't tomorrow yet. We would see then.

Tommy showed us to our room and we settled in. The room was painted bright blue and very clean, but extremely tiny. We would manage.

We were within easy walking distance of the town centre and started out to find a place to eat and imbibe. Tommy called us back just as we were leaving the yard and gave us a business card for T&G's. In case we got lost, we could just give this to someone and they'd see that we got home in one piece. He also mentioned that as long as it was still daylight, we could shorten our walk by cutting through the cemetery. He said he'd done it a few times, even after dark, and he'd come out unscathed. I don't think he was kidding. He recommended several places in town for dinner and relaxing and told us how to get there.

The walk through the cemetery was fairly interesting. The markers for all the Kellys, Fitzgeralds, and O'Brians ranged from a couple of centuries old to a week or so. The Irish seem to celebrate death more energetically than we do. The headstones we saw were much more dramatic and colourful than we're used to. I suppose that throughout their turbulent history, death was about the only thing the Irish could truly rely on, so they made the most of it.

You'd think that a five acre cemetery, and a level one at that, would be easy to navigate, but you wouldn't be counting on our unfailing ability to get lost. We got inside the wall without any difficulty, but we couldn't find a gate to get out on the other side. We finally found a gap in the wall, and ended up in a backyard. It didn't take long though to relocate the right street, and we were back on track.

Tommy had recommended a pub that served good food at reasonable prices. He called it something that sounded like "Chuck Dolman's." I thought that it was probably a place owned by a friend named Charles. We walked up and down the street for awhile looking for Chuck's sign, but couldn't see it. AHA! It finally hit me! Right across the street from where we were standing was a place with a sign reading **Teach Dolmen.** The Gaelic kicked in. *Teach* is pronounced something like "chakh" and it means house or place. So we were across the street from the Dolmen House, the place Tommy had recommended. Irish English, American English, and Gaelic—I thought we weren't going to have a language problem.

The interior of the place was quite distinctive. The ceiling is painted with all sorts of Celtic designs, reminiscent of the Book of Kells. There are some showcases around with Bronze Age artifacts displayed: mostly axe heads, spear points, and exquisitely crafted jewellery. It was a little noisier in here than most places, but there was a soccer match on TV, so that was that.

We ordered a starter of "Mini Salmon Tortillas" (a real cross-cultural mix, I'd say), which were actually quite tasty, followed by the special of the evening—roast lamb and vegetables, and of course potatoes. It was all very delicious, filling, and inexpensive. With the whole works washed down with a full pint of Guinness, we were hardly able to walk.

After our meal, we went back out on the street for a mini pub-crawl. It was a fine soft evening, and we had left our umbrellas in the car. A few doors up the street, we went into The Plough. The place had two bar areas, and we went into the small one. It was tiny, dark and old, just the place to take refuge from the weather. We each had a whiskey to settle the meal and watched a couple of the locals. These guys weren't the conversational types; they were the more contemplative Irish, gazing moodily into their pints and seemingly brooding on Ireland's sorrows. More likely, they had dropped the grocery money on a horse race and were afraid to go home.

Leaving the Plough, we crossed the street and went into the Saints and Sinners, where most of the furniture had been taken from a church, probably a Protestant one. (There's more than one way to beat 'em.) The benches were ornately carved pews, and a handsomely carved pulpit stood against one wall. I didn't see a confessional. It wasn't very crowded, and the barman was very friendly. It was a pretty relaxing place.

Our last stop for the evening was Reddy's, Tommy's favourite hangout. This was a more modern place, but still quiet and restful. We had our nightcap, chatted with the barman for awhile, and headed home.

It was still raining outside, but it was a gentle rain, nothing like a Minnesota summer downpour. We had the cemetery figured out by now and took the shortcut through it. We didn't encounter any banshees, pucas, or other supernatural beings, even though the atmosphere was right for it. I was a little disappointed. After all, if we had come all this way to walk at night through an Irish graveyard, you'd think we'd have at least got some screeching or bloody doom-filled curses for our efforts.

When we got back to our room, we discovered that the door couldn't be locked from the inside. The key just wouldn't work. While we were getting ready for bed, some other guest, by mistake, tried to use his key in the lock. I'm sure he just had the wrong room, but we piled all our luggage against the door as a barricade, just in case.

And so to bed. It was a long, eventful day—good food, excellent scenery, friendly people, and above all, world class bad navigating.

A VERY CIVIL DISTURBANCE

SEPTEMBER 15. We were up at 6:45 and immediately turned on the TV to get the latest news on the truckers' protest. Judging from all the reports, this was the biggest news story to hit Ireland in quite a while. Apparently this had been in the planning stages for months and was being put into motion to coordinate with similar actions in Britain and France. We'd seen these other protests on the news, and in some cases they had gotten pretty ugly.

RTE, the Irish television network, had reporters in place all over the country keeping everyone up to the minute on the protest. With growing apprehension, we watched a report that Carlow, as an important agricultural centre, would have its share of the protest. There was also a report from Rosslare Harbour that the protest there would be more intense, because of the shipping that goes through the port. Wonderful. Right where we're headed today.

However, there was a quite different attitude evident from the protestors who were being interviewed. In the US, when protestors of any sort are on camera, they generally carry on with fist waving, window smashing, rock throwing, obscenities and promises to shut everything down and to resort to whatever it takes to achieve their aims.

Here the truckers assured the public that they would try to inconvenience people as little as possible while getting their point across. Interviews with the *Gardai* gave much the same attitude. Apparently, the protest was going to be carried out after much detailed planning with law enforcement. In fact, it looked like the *Gardai* not only gave their permission for the protest, but even approved of it. After all, patrol cars use petrol too. So we were a little confused about what the day would bring, but we couldn't do much else except to go on with our plans and hope for the best.

I went outside to stretch a bit and see what was going on in the neighbourhood. As usual, there were a number of dogs nosing around here and there, and a few people puttering around in their yards. I struck up a conversation with a fellow next door who was out with his dog. The dog was a sassy little poodle type who first threatened to take off my leg and then decided that being petted was better. His owner bid me good morning and asked how we liked Ireland. He didn't know what to make of the big protest, but he didn't seem to be very concerned about it. He wished me an enjoyable trip and I went back in for breakfast.

After a walk downtown to change some money and get a phone card, we were packed up and ready to travel by 10:30. We got directions to Browne's Hill Dolmen, about three miles east of town, and headed out.

A dolmen is a type of Stone Age grave fairly common throughout the British Isles and in northern France. Dolmens usually are constructed of several upright stones over a burial chamber with a capstone placed somewhat horizontally across the uprights. They look something like a rough table. Archaeologists are still trying to figure out the construction method, as the capstone can be huge. The one at Browne's Hill Dolmen is estimated to weigh 100 tons.

We found the place without any difficulty. The dolmen is out in the middle of a sheep pasture and has a lane along a stone wall for a couple hundred yards leading out to it. The stone wall was in an interesting state of disrepair, with a lot of brambles growing out of it. Along the wall were a number of holly trees, heavily draped with ivy. Micki had been taking pictures off and on of holly trees and ivy vines along the way, but this was the first time we had seen the two growing together. I guess the concept is more than just a Christmas carol. We spent twenty minutes or so photographing the various combinations of the two.

We spent about a half-hour inspecting the dolmen. It hasn't been excavated yet, but there is an interpretive sign next to it explaining what is known about it. There is a burial beneath it, most likely a chieftain or king. There are taller uprights at the front of the structure with shorter ones behind them, so the massive capstone slants toward the back. The place is so undisturbed and natural that the creepy feeling of thin places is pretty strong.

There was a bunch of young Europeans at the site, and they asked me to take a picture of them in front of it. I did, but that wasn't our usual style. We generally took pictures of things as they are, without the intrusion of ourselves into the scene. We can take pictures of ourselves at home.

After the young folks left, we sat and contemplated for a bit, under the blank stares of the adjacent flock of sheep. The only disruption of this quiet rural Irish scene was the sound of air horns on a nearby highway. It seemed that the truckers were getting into the protest with a lot of enthusiasm. It was quite a contrast: a Stone Age tomb within earshot of a twenty first-century protest.

We left Carlow on N80 heading southeast toward Wexford and Rosslare Harbour. It was only 60 miles to our destination, so even with any delays caused by the protest, we thought we would be all right.

At 12:30 we stopped for a pint in Bunclody, a very pretty and picturesque town which actually has a wide street. It's in a sort of valley, and the highway widens out into two one-way streets with a substantial boulevard between them, planted with trees and flowerbeds. There is also ample parking, which was another surprise.

We easily found a little pub, Lennon's, to quench a terrible thirst with a half-pint. This is an unpretentious pub whose decor is knotty pine panelling with various kinds of key rings hung all over the place.

We headed down the road again toward Wexford. So far, we hadn't encountered any problems with the protest, but at Enniscorthy, things changed.

I suppose it was fitting that we should encounter protest at Enniscorthy. In the Irish rebellion of 1798, this area was the scene of the most savage fighting and the only place where the rebellion had any kind of success. A Wexford priest, Father John Murphy, led a poorly armed band of Croppy Boys to a brief victory at Boulavogue north of Enniscorthy. The victory was short-lived. Just a short time later, the Wexford rebels withstood a month long siege at Vinegar Hill just outside the city, but were eventually overrun.

Lord Cornwallis, the military governor of Ireland, was still smarting from his defeat at the hands of another gang of rebels twenty years before in the American colonies. He was not about to let another ragtag bunch repeat the humiliation, and his vengeance was brutal. He summarily hanged anyone remotely connected with the revolt, including those who had not actually taken up arms, but had only refused to denounce anyone suspected of it.

Father Murphy has since become a national hero. The official report on his death is that he was hanged for treason, but folk history claims that he was turned over to the Yeomen, the volunteer civilian Protestant cavalry who supported Cornwallis. The Yeos reputedly spent several days amusing themselves by torturing Murphy and then burning him alive before he died from the abuse. The irony of it all is that there were nearly as many Protestant Croppy Boys as there were Catholic.

Enniscorthy is long and narrow, lying parallel to the River Slaney. The highway goes right through town, and of course narrows down as it becomes the main street. About halfway through town, the road crosses over the river on an old narrow bridge, and it was here that the rebels of 2000 were carrying on their unique style of revolt.

We crawled long at a snail's pace all through town until we came to the left turn onto the bridge. Here it became obvious what the protestors were up to. They would form a group of about six trucks and drive very slowly across the bridge, then turn around and drive very slowly back across. However, this wasn't a continuous movement. After each crossing, they would pull over and let traffic through, then pull back into the pattern and repeat the crossing. They were keeping their word: they were just slowing down traffic to get attention, but not stopping it entirely.

When we got up to the turn, I noticed a number of truckers and several police officers standing in a group having coffee together. They didn't seem hostile to each other. I also noticed drivers wave to the truckers or give a thumbs up sign. This was certainly the mildest protest I'd ever heard of.

When we got across the bridge, we made a right turn to head south toward Wexford. Once we got out in the country again traffic was moving right along.

About fifteen miles south of Enniscorthy, just outside the city of Wexford, we recrossed the River Slaney at Ferrycarrig. We were just off the Atlantic here and the river was pretty wide. On the north side of the bridge was an old castle, and just opposite across the bridge was the Oak Tavern. It was 2:00 now and we hadn't had lunch. The place has a parking lot behind it right on the riverbank, so we pulled in for lunch and pictures. Micki took a few beautiful shots of the castle across the river, then we went in for a bite. It was busy but not overly crowded.

We had a very satisfying lunch: Micki had a roast beef plate and I had the roast pork loin. Meat seemed to be a lot more flavourful in Ireland. Maybe because most of it is locally produced on small farms where pigs can root and cows can graze to their hearts' content. It's probably fresher and less chemical laden, too.

After lunch, I called our B&B to get specific directions and check on the protest. I was told to simply follow N25 to Kilrane and we'd be right there. There didn't seem to be any protest activity going on, either.

We got to Kilrane at 3:00, and thanks to very clear directions, found Marienella Bed and Breakfast without a hitch. The house is set back from the road about fifty yards on a beautifully landscaped lot, screened from the road by a tall thick hedge. We checked in with Neil Carty, the owner, who assured us that we'd have no trouble with the ferry in the morning. He serves breakfast early so we could board the ferry in plenty of time. The harbour was visible from the yard, and it didn't look as big as I had thought it would.

We walked across the road to McFadden's, a small comfortable pub, and had a pint of cider, a nice alternative to Guinness. Cider is lighter, crisper, and fruitier, a good drink if you are really dry.

Nearly next door is the Kilrane Inn, which is a little more upscale than McFadden's but still comfortable. Before we went in, a convoy of trucks went by, headed for the harbour. An elderly lady (about my age) was standing out in the yard, cheering and waving them on. For a protest, this seemed to be pretty popular.

We went inside, got our drinks and sat down. Pretty soon the cheerleader came in and sat down at the bar. I went up for a refill and got to chatting with her. I didn't get much sense out of her, except that she seemed to be the local token bleeding heart liberal and supported every protest, whether she understood it or not. I didn't think she understood this one either.

There is an off-licence (off-sale) liquor shop attached to the pub, but it was closed. I asked the kid behind the bar when it would be open, and he told me that if I needed something, he'd open it right now. He got the key, opened the shop, and I bought a bottle of Three Stills, a brand of Irish whiskey I had never heard of before. It turned out to be very good: slightly heavier and sweeter than Jameson.

We headed back across the road to rest a little before dinner. The trucks were getting a little thicker now, and there were a lot of air horn serenades going on. We hoped this would settle down before tomorrow. We didn't want to be so close to the harbour and not be able to leave.

After an hour or so, we went back to the Kilrane Inn for dinner in their comfortable dining room off the bar area. We had the fish (cod) and chips with a Wexford cheddar cheese platter. It was, as usual, delicious and plentiful.

As we strolled back to Marienella, we noticed that trucks were pulling up and parking on both sides of the road. I hoped that this wasn't a bad sign for tomorrow. Just before dark I went outside to see what was going on. The trucks were parked bumper-to-bumper on both sides of the road, slowing on-going traffic considerably. As I was standing in the driveway watching, a driver pulled his truck right across the driveway entrance. There was a group of drivers standing around, so I waved to them in a sort of confused helpless way, hoping they'd get the picture about the driveway. They cheerfully waved back, but didn't do anything. Tomorrow could be difficult.

I went back in, sipped some Three Stills, watched TV and eventually crashed. For all the anxiety, it had been a pretty calm day. We hadn't been inconvenienced much by the protest, and most surprising of all, we didn't get lost once.

STRONGBOW'S ARCHERS

SEPTEMBER 16. We got up early today to have breakfast in time to make it down to the harbour to embark on the 8:30 ferry. After getting cleaned up, I went outside to check on the truck situation. There wasn't a truck in sight. Somehow, during the night, the truckers had all gone home. Well, after all, they had promised that it would be a 24-hour event, and they had kept their word.

We had a very delicious breakfast, packed up our stuff for the day trip to Wales, and headed out. The harbour was an easy mile from Marianella and wasn't congested at all. There is ample parking and a short walk across the parking lot to the terminal building.

Up a flight of stairs is the ticket counter where our tickets were waiting. We got the tickets, paid for them and followed the clerk's directions on how to board the ferry. There are two ferries that sail to Fishguard, Wales, out of Rosslare. One is a monstrous slow vessel that carries passengers, cars and semis full of freight and takes about 4 hours to make the trip. We had opted for the fast ferry, the Lynx, that carries passengers and automobiles. It's pretty good sized too, but has a speed boat type catamaran hull and travels about 45 mph. I don't know what kind of engines it has, but they must be powerful. A trip on the Lynx to Fishguard takes about 90 minutes.

After leaving the ticket desk and being advised to waste no time (which was surprising, considering the usual Irish pace), we had to travel a series of ramps and stairs, then board a bus for a short shuttle over to the boarding area. Apparently because of the car loading system, the Lynx can't be docked right next to the terminal. As we boarded the ferry, we could watch the tedious process of loading cars. It seemed that there was a line of cars three abreast about a block long. We congratulated ourselves that we were going on foot.

The Lynx is plenty comfortable, but not overly luxurious.

The passenger area is two floors high (I suppose I should call them decks) with a bar, restaurant, gift shop and change bureau. The seating area is roomy with chairs, tables and benches. The lower deck has a game room for kids with a good number of beeping and squawking arcade games.

We were ushered aboard by a contingent of crewmembers, both male and female, dressed in uniforms that looked right out of the fifties. The guys didn't look too bad, but the women's uniforms were badly in need of updating: calf length skirt, a sort of stewardess hat that hasn't been seen elsewhere since 1960, and a high buttoned jacket, the whole outfit a sort of moss green colour. However, they were an efficient, no nonsense bunch, and got everyone herded into their proper area in short order, and we were soon under way.

Once we cleared Rosslare Harbour, we could feel the engines throttle up and speed increase. Even with the size of the Lynx, getting one's sea legs took a while. The ocean wasn't particularly rough, but there was definite pitching and rolling. If you wanted to move around inside, you kept a handhold within reach: a seat, a rail or anything to keep your balance. I watched with helpless sympathy as a fellow passenger lost his balance and took a header down a short flight of stairs.

The weather was a typical mix of clouds and sun. I went out on the small observation deck to watch the Irish coast recede. With the speed of the ferry, it was quite windy and chilly out there. I didn't stay too long.

Why were we going to Wales anyway? Basically, of course, it would be an easy, interesting and inexpensive day trip, and it is another Celtic country. Beyond that, though, our ancestors likely came from there. When I was a little kid, my Aunt Julia told me once, in tones that suggested some dark family secret, that her family was not really Irish; they were originally Welsh, hence the name. Sometime, apparently centuries ago, according to Aunt Julia, an ancestor or two moved to Ireland from Wales. The locals just called them the Welsh, and it became the family name. The same name is also spelled Walsh, and in Ireland the two names are somewhat interchangeable.

I did some superficial research on this before we left the US and found a fairly complicated linguistic situation. Are you ready for a stuffy history lecture?

Most of the island of England was conquered by the Romans in about 40AD and remained a Roman province for about 400 years. There were several legions stationed there, and over the decades became filled with local men, who, although Roman citizens, had never been off the island. The Roman system of military pensions was to grant land to 20-year veterans, usually in the place they had been stationed. So veterans of the Roman army established villas and farms on the Roman pattern and remained loyal and productive citizens of Rome, even though ethnically they were Celtic. The culture gradually became a mixture of Roman and Celtic.

When the Dark Ages began, Rome severed ties with Britain and declared it to be a free country, since other parts of the overextended empire needed defence against barbarian tribes invading from the north. Rome pulled its military out of Britain, leaving it practically defenceless against any invasion.

In the middle 400's AD, invaders from northwest Germany started arriving in Britain, at first just to plunder, eventually to settle. The Roman/Celtic inhabitants put up a valiant but futile defence (the origin of the King Arthur legend), but were eventually driven to the remote southwest corner of the island.

The Germanic invaders were known as Saxons, and are the ancestors of the modern English. In their language, they called the defeated natives *Waelsa,* which simply means outsiders. The "outsiders" in their own land referred to themselves as *Cymru* (pronounced like "kim-ree") derived from *Cambria,* the Latin name for the area.

The Saxons eventually settled most of Britain, but left the territory of the *Cymru* alone. For the next few centuries, there was an uneasy peace between the two peoples, as the Saxons consolidated their territories into one kingdom.

In 1066, William of Normandy in northern France, a descendant of Vikings, laid claim to the throne of England, as Britain was now known. After one decisive battle at Hastings, William became king of England and began a ruthless reorganization of the country. The Saxons were now a defeated population and were subjected to Norman law and custom. The *Cymru* were now known as Welsh to the rest of the island, and their territory was known as Wales.

The Welsh had little strength to resist the Normans, and Celts that they were, held a long standing grudge against the Saxons and were basically indifferent to their defeat. Within a few decades, most of England, including Wales, was divided up into various duchies, baronies, earldoms and other feudal territories, all technically loyal to the king.

In 1170, Dermot McMurrough, a contender for the high kingship of Ireland, called on Henry II of England to aid his cause. Henry had long been looking for an excuse to invade Ireland and jumped at his chance. He dispatched Richard FitzGilbert de Clare, nicknamed Strongbow, and Earl of Pembroke in Wales to go to Dermot's aid.

Although de Clare was a Norman knight, his invasion force probably contained a large contingent of Welsh archers. These masters of the longbow were considered the most deadly military force of the time, reputedly able to send a three-foot arrow 300 yards with uncanny accuracy.

Strongbow invaded Ireland, established Dermot as a sort of puppet, married his daughter, and stayed on with his army. He built castles and cathedrals and eventually with a number of fellow Normans and their armies, became established in Ireland, adopting the country as their own and adapting to Irish language and customs.

The Welsh archers stayed on too, and being commoners, married into the native population. They were called Welsh by the English and *Brannagh* (foreigners) by the Gaelic speaking Irish. The names stuck and now Welsh (or Walsh) and Brannagh are common Irish surnames. I would like to imagine that sometime 800 years ago, my ancestors were part of Strongbow's army that originated in Pembrokeshire, Wales, where Fishguard is situated.

And that's why we were going to Wales.

We spent most of the trip across the Celtic Sea sipping coffee and doing crossword puzzles. There was a computerized map on a TV monitor in the passenger lounge that showed our position and progress. As the Welsh coast came into view, I went out onto the deck and got to chatting with a guy. He asked me where I was from and, as usual, if I had any connection to Ireland. I told him that my grandfather had his roots in West Cork, to which he replied that he lived in West Cork and wanted to know what the family name was. I told him it was Welsh, and he said that that was his own name. We agreed that the connection was probably rather slim, given that we were short on facts. However, as he went inside, he wished me a good trip and remarked, "You know, we just *could* be cousins."

As the ferry was being moored, a rather lengthy process, passengers were directed over the PA to go to the disembarking area of the vessel. We managed to end up in the hold where the cars were parked. We found our way out of there easily enough, and it was a relief getting the daily "getting lost" routine over with early.

The port at Fishguard is rather small. There is a terminal building with rail and highway connections to the rest of the country, but little else right close. The village of Fishguard is located a couple of miles from the port on the top of a sizable cliff. It was plainly visible from the terminal, and very picturesque, but it was too far to walk, and we had no idea how to get there.

There were some other people who had gotten off the ferry with us, and we now saw them walking toward a petrol station and a few other buildings about a quarter mile away. We figured they might know what they were doing, so we followed behind them. I don't know whether they previously knew it or not, but there was a bus stop right across from the petrol station. We stood around a bit, and a bus came along. The driver told us this bus went right up to the centre of Fishguard, so we hopped on and rode up to the village in about five minutes.

Dickens would have loved Fishguard. Maybe he did. I don't care for the patronizing term "quaint," but Fishguard comes close to that description. It has a town square with little narrow crooked streets running off in every direction. Apparently Fishguard (*Abergwaun* in Welsh) isn't on any major route, so what little traffic there was in town was mostly local folks.

We went to a very well furnished tourist centre right on the town square and got the local bus schedule. We wanted to find out when the bus went back to the port, so we could organize our day in time to get back for our 4:00 return trip to Ireland.

The thirst was upon us, and we found the Coach House Inn quite handy. Being of open mind and strictly scientific attitude, we entered to sample the local beverages. Worthington Ale is a local Welsh favorite, with a nickname I didn't catch. It's a creamy spicy pale ale that is served quite a bit warmer than beer in Ireland. Micki spotted Strongbow Cider on tap and ordered a pint. We were in Pembrokeshire after all and Micki has a well-developed sense of the sweep of history, and sometimes a powerful thirst.

Before we left the town square, I noticed a bank open for business. I had brought some travellers' checks in Sterling (English currency) so we went in to cash a few. I didn't think it would be a problem since there was no foreign money involved. The teller refused to cash them because we weren't "regular customers." I thought of pulling the old Stephan Leacock (a Canadian humorist) trick in dealing with intimidating bank tellers: open a savings account, deposit £10, and then immediately draw out everything but 5p. With electronic banking today, the irritation factor wouldn't be as great as in Leacock's time, but I thought about it. Well, I suppose the teller was only following bank policy, but it was annoying, nevertheless. The pubs in town cashed them readily, as long as we made a purchase.

We headed up a street and discovered a farmers' market in the parking lot of a grocery store. All the local farmers and gardeners regularly bring their produce in here to sell. If Americans would just get over their fetish about packaged food and get into this system of local markets, both the cuisine and the farm economy would improve considerably.

We strolled around a bit, tried some samples, and fell into a conversation with a local sheep farmer who was selling his own farm-made cheese. He graciously offered us some samples, knowing very well we really weren't going to be paying customers. He had several varieties, and they were delicious. He asked us if we had come over from Rosslare on the Lynx. When we told him we had, he asked how the trip was. We told him that it had been quite comfortable and enjoyable.

He got into telling us about how when the Lynx was first put into service, quite recently I guess, trips were very frequently cancelled because of rough weather. It sounded like that at the slightest hint of rough seas, the Lynx stayed in port. The locals on both sides, Welsh and Irish, dubbed the ferry "The Olympic Flame," because it never went out. Frequent passengers on the Lynx have also named it the "Vomit Comet." You can figure that out without explanation.

We left the open-air market and headed back to the town centre. On the way we stopped into the Ship & Anchor, for another ale and cider. This is an old fashioned place where the ales aren't pressurized. They've got the old style hand pumps with big polished brass handles. The whole place had a nice old nautical atmosphere.

Two doors down the street is Bennett's Navy Tavern. We stepped in here for some more scientific sampling. The barman in here was a very conversational guy. Micki being a cider aficionado by now ordered a brand of cider called Scrumpy Jack, a local cider made fairly close to Fishguard. This got the barman launched into a long dissertation about cider. Local apple farmers are nicknamed scrumpies and the cider they make is called scrumpy jack (like applejack). Scrumpy Jack evolved into a folk character who isn't too bright and is the subject of numerous bad jokes, and is now the brand name of a popular type of cider.

I had ordered a Boddington's Ale, something I hadn't tried before. While the barman was giving his cider lecture, he was also drawing my ale. He drew about half a pint and then let the glass sit to let the head settle. He was really warming up to his subject and we were both pretty engrossed in his story. When he finished filling my pint, he was on to other topics. I took a sip out of it and it seemed to have a very pronounced apple taste. I hadn't noticed this, but Micki had: when he was telling his cider story, he took my half filled glass and inadvertently filled it up with cider. He was yakking away and never realized what he was doing. I didn't say anything about it because I didn't want to embarrass the guy into silence—he was pretty entertaining. I was going to have to wait to find out about Boddington's Ale.

The next topic the barman got into was the state of medicine in Britain. Whenever Micki mentioned that she was a nurse, we usually got some unique slant on the local state of health care, disease, the perfidy of doctors, the bungling government, or any other topic remotely related to medicine. It was usually pretty enlightening, kind of a grassroots take on things that don't make into the newspapers.

Our man got into the subject of medicine in general by telling us about his case of labyrinthitis. This meant nothing to me, but Micki knew what he was talking about: it's a condition of severe vertigo and balance problems. He gave us some pretty vivid descriptions of his episodes—falling down stairs, double vision, and the room whirling around him. I was starting to get a little queasy.

He then got warmed up about medical specialists and the incompetence of MD's in general. He told us that doctors in England were recently given a test, and less than half of them knew how to do CPR. Nothing gets people ranting like medicine, government, or insurance companies. In Britain, with National Health Service, it's pretty convenient: you can whack all three at once in one grand tirade.

This was all quite entertaining, but our time was limited. As we were leaving, the barman told us not to miss the tapestry display. We had seen signs about it all over town, but weren't too sure what it was. We'd have to check it out. We went back to the town centre, found the tapestry display in a church hall and went in to look at it. It's quite a piece of work.

A little background might help here. When the Normans invaded and conquered England in 1066, the ladies of the Norman nobility in France put together a magnificent piece of stitchery to commemorate the event. Known as the Bayeaux Tapestry, It is a strip of cloth 20 inches wide by 200 feet long. It depicts all the events of the Norman invasion in a series of pictures all done in exquisite needlework, a sort of medieval storyboard.

Now the Fishguard Tapestry is a rural Welsh depiction of an invasion of Fishguard in 1797. In that year, during the long sporadic series of wars between England and France, a small French fleet sailed into Fishguard harbour with the intent of doing some minor mayhem and looting. It seemed that they had been sailing around for some months without accomplishing anything, and they couldn't go home without at least a token victory. Napoleon or whoever was in power would be highly displeased, so the fleet commander decided that an attack on Fishguard would be easy pickings, since the only defenders were a bunch of Welsh farmers who wouldn't put up much resistance.

The French, being the well-fed but stupid perverts that they are (remember, this is the local version now), made a big mistake. They were met at the shore by a mob of enraged Welshmen, led by a very frightening woman named Jemimah. In a matter of a few minutes, the Welsh had beaten the French invaders into submission with clubs, rocks and pitchforks, and herded them up into the town and kept them under guard while someone went to inform the nearest English military authority.

A French soldier tried to organize a breakout, but the rest of them mobbed him and cut his throat to shut him up. Apparently they had had enough combat for now.

The English authorities arrived and negotiated a surrender, somewhat unnecessarily, considering that the French were already beaten into submission and were not inclined to rekindle the wrath of Jemimah and her gang of patriots, but this was the eighteenth century, and war had a certain amount of etiquette attached to it. The articles of surrender were signed at the Royal Oak Inn, a number of ceremonies were performed, and the French were hauled back down to their anchored ships, and told to stay the hell out of Fishguard.

Now all this took place in 1797, and on the two hundredth anniversary of the event, the modern citizens of Fishguard decided to commemorate the invasion by stitching a pictorial tapestry just like the Bayeaux Tapestry recalled the Norman Conquest. The result is displayed in St. Mary's church hall. It is a truly marvellous piece of craftsmanship, but there is a definite tongue-in-cheek attitude about it. Jemimah is pictured as this huge mean looking woman with a big stick. The French are pictured as cowardly little weasels, and the English authorities who finally show up are portrayed as clueless and bumbling. I'm glad we got to take a look at it. History books leave a lot out.

We went back to the town centre and went to the Royal Oak Inn for lunch. Yep, the very same spot where the French were forced to surrender. It didn't look like the interior had changed much in two centuries. Curry dishes are quite popular in the British Isles, since so many ordinary citizens spent time in the military in India during the Empire's glory days of the nineteenth century and brought back a taste for Asian food. I had a beef curry, and Micki ordered the lamb and leek curry. They were delicious, savoury without being overpowering.

There were several American tourists in the place, just off a tour bus, and were trying to decide on lunch. I won't go into their behaviour right now. That deserves a special treatment of its own.

We did a little shopping around the town, mostly in a small shop where a young guy, who apparently was fluent in both Gaelic and Welsh, gave us a few pointers on Welsh pronunciation. I bought a tape on the Welsh language, which isn't as difficult as the written form looks, and Micki bought some jewelry and craft items.

We had time for one more pub visit before the bus took us back to the harbour. We stopped at the Abergwaun (pronounced Aber-gwine) Hotel for a last ale and cider. It wasn't too distinguished a place, but it was adequate.

We caught the bus in plenty of time, and it dropped us off at the petrol station where we had boarded in the morning. We still had a quarter mile walk back to the terminal. When we got close to the building, an electronic sign informed us that the Lynx was running about 45 minutes behind schedule. We sat out our time in the bar at the terminal, at a window table with a good view of the harbour. Seagulls brazenly begged for handouts just outside the glass. We had a nice view of the Lynx pulling up to the pier and docking.

There weren't nearly as many people heading back to Rosslare, so the boarding process was pretty quick. As we were heading up the ramp to get aboard, one of the crew yelled out to the passengers, "Anybody here know how to drive a boat?" All Celts are aspiring comedians.

Once everyone was aboard, the ferry headed out to the open sea. I was out on the deck watching the receding shoreline and trying to get a decent picture. All of a sudden, there was a splash in the water right below me. A big dolphin had jumped out of the water and into the air about six feet and then started outrunning the ferry. He was far too fast to get a picture. I called Micki out onto the deck, and we did manage to watch a school of dolphins jumping around a couple of hundred yards behind us. It was quite a sight; I'd never seen that before.

The return to Rosslare was so uneventful as to be boring. About the only outstanding thing about it was that I managed to go to the bar and get a Boddington's Ale undiluted by cider.

After we disembarked at Rosslare, We headed back to Marianella. On the way we stopped at a tourist centre and booked a B&B in Carrick-on-Suir, County Tipperary, for the next night. We also picked up a Collins Road Atlas, which has a very detailed depiction of roads. We could have used this a lot earlier in the trip.

After unloading our treasures in our room, we crossed the street to McFadden's for a light supper. We got a cold meat and cheese plate, a salad and a basket of brown bread. At the bar next to us was a local guy who was entertaining the tourists by being the quintessential stage Irishman. He had a tweed cap, a well-worn collarless shirt, and a brown jacket, a pipe and a two-day beard. Behind the bar was a well done crayon portrait of himself, and his act was to sit in approximately the same pose as his picture, until someone recognized that he and the portrait were the same guy. Invariably, visitors would give a little start when they saw the connection. Then he'd get into a conversation with them. It seemed that this was the nightly entertainment in the place.

After supper, we tried to call home, but the phone in McFadden's wouldn't connect, and the phone booth outside was out of order. This was the first time we'd had any problem with the phone system. Normally, it's pretty efficient. We recrossed the road and retired for the night. This was probably the biggest day so far: an ocean voyage, another foreign country, new kinds of beer, and dolphins jumping around. Hard to beat that.

ANNE BOLEYN'S CHAIR

SEPTEMBER 17. We arose at a comfortable time and enjoyed a leisurely breakfast. Today we were headed for Carrick-on-Suir, the hometown of the Clancy Brothers. We have had the good fortune to share a drink and some conversation with Liam, Bobby, and the late beloved Pat, so today was almost a sort of pilgrimage.

Most of today's ferry passengers at Marianella had already eaten and left, so there were just us and another couple at breakfast. The brown bread was particularly good, and the other couple was raving about it. Neal was rather pleased, because it sounded as if he had baked it himself today. He had the recipe stored in his computer, and he very graciously ran off some copies of it for us. We've tried it since we've gotten home and it is just as delicious here.

We got on the road at 9:00 and headed for Waterford. It was Sunday and there was very little traffic. The day was misty with some fog up around the tops of hills. It wasn't gloomy or depressing, but rather mysterious and awe-inspiring. We had purchased some CD's of Welsh male choirs, and since Clio had an excellent CD player, we fulfilled our Sunday obligation by listening to *Rho i mi hen ffydd fy nhadau* (Give Me That Old Time Religion). It was more satisfying than sitting in a church.

We stopped outside of Waterford at a little layby right on the River Suir. There was an old ruined castle just across the river from where we were parked. We first assumed that this was Reginald's Tower but later found out that that castle is in the centre of

Waterford. Whatever this castle was called, it was impressive. It had a wall that ran right down into the water and what looked liked an entrance gate in it. We took a few pictures and headed up the road to Carrick.

Carrick is a medium sized town of 5000, but very old. It was only 11:00 when we arrived, and on a Sunday, there wasn't too much happening. We did the only thing possible—find a pub. We went into the Carrick Hotel where Crotty's Pub is located. Pubs can be open on Sunday morning, but no liquor can be served until 12:30. We had to content ourselves with a cup of tea.

Since we had a lot of time to kill, we went out on the street and looked for Ormond Castle. It was only about three blocks away from the hotel, so we walked up there to check it out.

There is a tall iron fence around the place, and when we checked the gate, we found it locked. As we were standing there wondering what to do next, a couple drove up and also checked the gate. The guidebooks had said the place was open into September, but it was all quiet and dark.

As we four were standing there contemplating our next move, a little car drove up and a small old guy got out and walked up to us. We asked him about the hours of the place, and we immediately got into one of the most amazing experiences of the trip.

The little old guy introduced himself as the curator of the place. Indeed he had grown up in a part of the castle, and although he couldn't give us a tour, he could open it up and let us look around on our own.

For the next ninety minutes, he escorted us through the whole place. For someone who couldn't give a tour, he certainly gave us a pretty good imitation of one. His name was Michael Wallace; "The real Mike Wallace," although he had been contacted by the one in the US who reads the news, who had heard about his Irish namesake. Michael's great-grandfather had been the gardener for the Butler family one hundred fifty years ago. His family had been connected with the estate in one way or the other ever since. The Butlers, and there are still some of them around, were the Dukes of Ormond and had some very prominent positions in the British nobility in the sixteenth and seventeenth century.

Apparently, their prosperity was based on the family ability to join up with whichever political or religious faction held power at the moment. It sounded like the Butlers had been Catholic, Anglican, Royalist, Puritan, Stuart, and Hanoverian whenever the situation called for it.

The castle itself is built in three sections. The first castle, built in 1309, was erected by the Normans who needed a central stronghold to control the rich lands of Tipperary and the transportation route on the River Suir. They got control by the simple expedient of burning every building for miles around and slaughtering anyone who got in their way.

The original castle was built right on the banks of the Suir, with a portion of the wall extending right into the river. A gate was built on the river, (actually right in the river) so that boats could be brought right into the courtyard of the castle. This type of structure was the origin of the term "Watergate," which has a far different connotation in the US.

The second portion of the castle was built in 1450. It was actually an addition onto the first, but built somewhat higher in elevation. From the looks of it, the river level had changed and the watergate was now on solid ground, making its original purpose useless.

The third and newest section of the castle was built by Black Tom Butler in the time of Elizabeth I. According to Michael, Black Tom built the house in the hopes that Elizabeth would come to Ireland for a visit, a sort of Renaissance "Field of Dreams,"—If I build it, she will come. Apparently, she never did. This portion is very well preserved, and is the part of the property where Michael grew up. His family's living quarters were in the Tudor house, and, as he told us, the older portion of the castle was a great place to play cowboys and Indians. (The Lone Ranger and Tonto in County Tipperary—mind boggling.)

Our tour started at the front door of the Tudor house. The other couple with us was a doctor from Indiana and his wife, very nice people. The doctor was pretty well versed on history and architecture, without being snobby or obnoxious. Michael showed us some frescoes in the lower hall depicting Queen Elizabeth I and Black Tom Butler, Duke of Ormond, evidently painted during their lifetimes. He said that there is a convincing amount of evidence that Ormond and Elizabeth were lovers and that Elizabeth had a child by him. I remarked that the present English monarchy then were really impostors. Michael's attitude was that it didn't make much difference—they were all nitwits.

Michael went into great detail about the plaster on the walls, a mixture of lime, sand and horsehair, and the use of dead horses under the floorboards for soundproofing. We never asked about the effect of the aroma of rotting horseflesh in the kitchen, but I'd guess that in those days, rotten smells were pretty much part of the atmosphere.

Suddenly there was a knock on the main door. Michael quickly directed us to hide in a short hallway. The place was supposed to be closed, and there was no telling what would happen if we were discovered. With a great deal of drama and the four of us cowering in the little hallway, he went to a front window and yelled out to whoever was out there that the place was closed for the season and that there was absolutely nobody around. "Nobody! Do you hear?"

After this little comedy, we were guided out the back of the house into the blended courtyards of the previous castles. There has been some restoration over the years but some controversy about how much should be done. Michael's opinion seemed to be that 1) the government was underfunding the project and 2) the people in charge of restoration were wasting what they got.

The medieval castles have not only suffered the ravages of time and weather. Like a lot of old buildings in Ireland, Cromwell trashed Castle Ormond on his infamous campaign in Ireland in the 1650's. Evidently in his divine mission to send all Papists to "hell or Connaught," he encountered some resistance at Ormond. He shelled the 1309 segment of the castle, eventually blowing a hole in the wall on the river side. Once his troops gained entrance, he seized the place and used it as headquarters for control of the area. He left the Tudor house relatively unscathed, as he found it useful as a barracks for his men.

We spent a good half-hour exploring the courtyards. Michael pointed out a number of features that we wouldn't have recognized otherwise. Parts of the towers built in 1450 had collapsed over time, exposing staircases and remnants of fireplaces where sleeping quarters were located. Since we were at the back of the Tudor house, Michael also showed us the remnants of kitchen and storage areas, giving us a glimpse of the routine daily activities of 500 years ago.

The next stage of the "non-tour" was an examination of the upper floors of the Tudor house. Our talkative guide let us in through an old door, using the original key to open it.

We went up a very narrow winding staircase that led to the private quarters of Thomas Butler. The original furnishings are all in place, with only a minimum amount of restoration. The original oak flooring is very sound, but the decorative plaster friezes along the corners where the walls join the ceiling have had some work done on them. Michael told us that when he was a kid, occasionally he would hear a clunk when he was downstairs, and he would go up and find that a piece of the carved plaster had fallen from the ceiling. He saved all the broken pieces over the years and when the time came to restore the rooms, the restorers had the original work to make new plaster moulds for exact duplicates.

Black Tom Butler's quarters contained a sitting room with a fireplace and bookshelves and a larger room with the original canopy bed. There is some speculation that Ann Boleyn, Henry VIII's second wife, was born at Ormond Castle. If that were true, she would have to have been born in the 1450 section of the castle, since the Tudor house wasn't built until the time of her daughter Elizabeth. Michael discounted the story of Anne Boleyn being born at Ormond, but he is convinced that she did spend a good deal of time here. That would make the supposed affair of Black Tom and Elizabeth more plausible.

The mental picture I have of Anne Boleyn is Genevieve Bujold, the Canadian actress who played Anne in the excellent film adaptation of Maxwell Anderson's powerful poetic drama *Anne of a Thousand Days*. My view of her is a flirtatious innocent who got in over her head in the ruthless complex world of Tudor politics. Henry VIII's obsessive desire for a male heir overrode the bounds of sanity, and Anne was his first tragic victim. It is an extreme irony of history that after she was executed on a flimsy charge of treason, her daughter Elizabeth I became the most powerful monarch in her day, but the last Tudor.

There were some pieces of original furniture in Butler's quarters—dressers, chairs, and even a cradle. Michael invited us to sit in a chair that he said Ann Boleyn had undoubtedly used. If that were the case, the chair would have to have been over 550 years old and come from the 1450 castle. We were all a little hesitant about possibly wrecking such a priceless antique, but the temptation to touch history got the best of us and we all gave it a try. It was an indescribable feeling to make that connection with the past. Imagine sitting in a chair where Anne Boleyn's cute little butt had once parked.

The other room we visited was the Great Hall on the third floor. This was a sort of ballroom sized reception area that was apparently used for affairs of state. This room runs nearly the entire length of the house and has been pretty thoroughly restored. The entire original row of windows (including the glass) is all in place and let a good deal of daylight into the room.

Michael asked us at this point if any of us were fishermen. We were rather noncommittal at this, not knowing where it was leading. He then asked us if we knew what a Carrick knot was. I remembered having learned to tie it when I was a Boy Scout. Michael finally asked us to look at the ceiling. We looked up and the cornices of the room were decorated with plaster friezes of Carrrick knots alternated with clusters of oak leaves. Michael explained that the Carrick knot (or bend, as it is sometimes called) originated right there in Carrick-on-Suir in the early Middle Ages by fishermen on the River Suir. It developed into a symbol of the area and worked its way into heraldry and decoration. Today it can be found all over the district in various forms of artwork.

Micki asked Michael about the significance of oak leaves, as we had seen that motif in quite a few places. He explained that it really went all the way back to pre-Christian times when Druids carried on their ceremonies in oak groves. At one time, Ireland was covered with oak forests, and called our attention to the centuries old flooring we were standing on. When the English came, they deforested the country, using the oak for shipbuilding. Today, there is very little oak left on the island.

We ended our tour at that point. Micki had been taking videotape throughout the whole thing. Michael put on a big expression of feigned surprise when he found out what she had been doing. He said he'd like to see himself on camera, but he couldn't figure out how to be in the picture and look at the viewfinder at the same time. I had been taking pictures all through the tour and Michael said he didn't mind, but he cautioned us not to have them developed in Ireland, because pictures were not allowed in the castle and if anyone found out about our unauthorized tour, he'd be in big trouble.

We bid Michael Wallace a fond and extremely grateful goodbye. You hear of Irish luck, but I was getting to believe there is something to it. If we had been at the gate of Ormond Castle thirty seconds later than we were, we'd have missed one of the most enjoyable parts of our trip.

It was still early, so we found a phone booth and called Dan and Santina. We probably didn't make much sense. I think we were still high on the Ormond Castle experience, with our heads still floating around in the Middle Ages.

We had worked up a powerful thirst by this time, so we headed across the street to the Comeragh Bar. It was nice enough, but the loud blaring of rock music from their CD player shattered the traditional atmosphere. At the least, it brought us back to the twenty first century.

We left the Comeragh after a half-pint and recrossed the street. As we were walking up the street, we passed a bureau de change, a little office that changes currency. Since it was Sunday, it wasn't open, but there was a fellow working on the doorframe. We stopped to chat with him, and he told us that he was trying to get the door in better shape before business hours the next day. We told him that we'd probably see him tomorrow when he was open. Almost next door is the Tir Na nOg (Gaelic for Land of the Young, the Celtic paradise), a very small place with stone walls inside, and very much quieter than the Comeragh. It was a nice place, but they don't serve food, and we were starting to get hungry.

We went back out on the street and headed for a place called Moore's, which had a sign outside stating that they serve bar snacks. It was a little shabby and seemed to have its regulars: the place had a lot of little kids running around and a couple of guys were playing darts over the heads of the rug rats. The barmaid didn't seem to know anything about the sign outside, which was all right, because we decided we didn't want to eat in there anyway.

We left Moore's and headed back to the Carrick Hotel. It was only about 3:30, but the day had been so full already that it seemed like we had been there for quite a while. The Carrick was still serving their "carvery," so we decided to eat there. A carvery is a sort of buffet luncheon that is very common in pubs on Sunday. It is the Irish version of a Sunday brunch. It generally consists of several types of roasts, along with your choice of vegetables and dessert. The choices today were roast beef or roast pork loin. We both had the pork and roasted potatoes; Micki had the carrots, and I had Brussels sprouts. As usual, there was a lot of it, and it was delicious. We took our meal to the table we had occupied when we first hit town and leisurely enjoyed it.

We followed up our meal with a Hennessey and a cup of coffee, and sat for a while watching the locals filter in. It was a fine soft day outside, and people were drifting in to watch a semi-final hurling match on the telly. Evidently, this is a weekly ritual. People come in with their kids and dogs, and rearrange the chairs and tables so everyone has a good view of the screen. They all order food or drinks and while away a Sunday afternoon.

I didn't understand all the intricacies of the game, but hurling seems to be some way of settling old grudges in a semi-organized way. The game is a version of field hockey or lacrosse, and it is a very ancient game. The old pre-Christian Celtic legends mention it quite frequently. A hard leather ball about the size of a baseball is batted around by two teams wielding weapons (called camanns) that look like hockey sticks, but with wider, rounder blades. The object is to knock the ball into a soccer-like net to make a point. The ball can be hit and passed on the ground, but can also be hit through the air. It may also be carried by a running player who dribbles it upward into the air with his camann as he runs. If the opportunity presents itself, the player with the ball knocks it high into the air and when it comes down, he winds up and gives it a whack, either passing it to a team mate or toward the goal. If there is somebody behind him during his back swing, there is a definite possibility of getting a good smack in the teeth. It is the defence's duty to gain control of the ball, apparently using any tactic that works. There are no timeouts or replacements, and injured players are dragged off the field, hopefully before they get trampled. Hurling seems to use all the murderous elements of every team sport and mould them into an afternoon of carnage and destruction. The Irish love it.

The bar was getting pretty crowded as the match on TV progressed. We didn't quite understand what we were watching, so we settled up and left, leaving more room for the locals. We returned to the phone booth on the street where we had called home before, and put in a call to Steve and Laurice. While Micki was on the phone, I watched a little scruffy tan dog making his way down the opposite side of the street. It was still raining, and he'd sit in a doorway until someone came by with an umbrella. Then he'd walk with them under the umbrella to the next doorway. Here he'd wait for another umbrella to come along and then use its shelter to get to the next door. He was making his trip down the street this way.

Micki talked for a while and then I took the phone. While I was gabbing, Micki spotted a sort of Dairy Queen shop and went in and got a huge cone. When I hung up, I tasted it. It was pretty tasty and only cost 40p.

We'd been hanging around these several blocks on Carrick's main street for a couple of hours now, but we still hadn't hit all the pubs. We crossed the street yet again and went into Pollard's. We'd had such a heavy meal that a Guinness wasn't that appealing, so we each had a half-pint of cider. I was having trouble getting the right change out of the pile of coins in my pocket, so the lady behind the bar said, "Och, just go sit down and enjoy your drink. You can figure it out there." That's what I liked about rural Ireland: everyone treats you like you'd been there all your life.

As we were enjoying our cider, the little dog that had run the umbrella game came in the door. He was slightly wet, and took one look at all the people in the place and immediately went into the poor pathetic orphan dog act. He shook himself off and went over to a radiator and settled himself down in front of it with a big sigh. It was the great classic sigh of Irish martyrdom. Even the dogs got it down.

We left Pollard's and headed for our lodging for the evening. We had booked this place, Fatima House, in Rosslare last night. We were a little concerned about the name of the place; for all we knew, it might be some kind of retreat house or a Virgin Mary shrine or a marathon rosary headquarters. I had visions of nuns chanting all night and keeping us awake. Without any difficulty, we found it only a few blocks away.

We needn't have worried about any religious excesses at Fatima House, although we never did discover the reason for the name. It is a very well kept older house run by Dick and Nuala Gaul. They are extremely nice people. Nuala is a quiet, dignified lady, and Dick would like to give you the impression that he is a complete lunatic. He pretty well succeeds. As we were getting our room and house keys, we got to chatting about the Clancy Brothers, the hometown boys. We mentioned that we had met Pat, Bobby and Liam. Nuala suggested that we call up Bobby, as he lives right in town, and ask him to show us around. We were nonplussed by this, but apparently he does this quite frequently. It seemed that Dick and Nuala were not particularly impressed by the Clancys' fame; they were proud of them, of course, but they were just local boys that happened to have a bit of good luck.

Dick then gave us the house rules: there was to be no staggering in at 4:00 AM singing "Country Roads." He didn't have any objection to 4 o'clock, staggering or singing, but he hated "Country Roads." This sounded to me like a not too subtle warning to avoid acting too American.

Dick showed us to our room and a beautiful room it was. It was on two levels and full of antique furniture. He pointed out the coffee maker and fixings (a standard feature at most B&B's) and cautioned us to go easy on the milk or he'd have to go out and chase down the goat. I wondered how many times a week he pulled this on visitors, and how many of them believed it.

We settled in and caught up on our notes in the logbooks. This had been a most adventurous day, and the evening hadn't begun yet. We debated about calling up Bobby Clancy, but we chickened out. Dick had told us that Bobby likes to hang out at the Old Mill pub, so we compromised and decided we might run into him there.

We started to leave the house at 7:30, but got waylaid by Dick at the door. He regaled us with a few stories and recommended the Park Inn as a good place to eat. Carrick is not very big in area, so we set out on foot for the evening pub-crawl. It looked like it might rain, but then it always looks that way in Ireland. It was quite warm, and I left my jacket behind. Micki took her heavy Aran sweater in case it turned cooler. We left the umbrellas in the car.

As we approached the first pub up the street, the Kickham Inn, a little car pulled up to the curb, and a young woman got out of the driver's seat and helped a very old guy out of the back seat. She took a walker out of the boot, got the old guy situated with it on the sidewalk, and drove off. By this time, we were already at the bar, and the old guy made his way slowly into the place and went to a table in the middle of the room. The four or five people in there all greeted him (his name was Tom) and the bartender brought him two hefty glasses of Paddy and lemonade, the Irish term for what we would call 7Up. Tom lit up a cigarette and started in on his drinks.

There was an evening soap opera on TV, and everyone in the place was making comments about it, mostly sarcastic ones. We got to chatting with a guy who had a guitar case and a bag full of sheet music with him. He told us he'd be playing here later on and invited us to come in and enjoy the music.

We told him that we probably would and got ready to leave. Old Tom was on his fourth Paddy and lemonade by this time. There was enough Paddy in his drinks to knock out a walrus. Everybody in the place kept an eye on him to make sure he was okay. Evidently, the place is sort of an assisted drinking establishment for old people. I just may retire there.

The Old Mill, Bobby Clancy's reputed hangout, was just up the street. We found it without difficulty, got our pints, and checked the place all over to see if our man was in there. No luck. There were a few blue-haired matrons sitting around and some young guys in the back, but nary a Clancy in sight. Maybe there was, since they're a pretty big tribe, but we didn't recognize anyone.

Slightly disappointed, we drank up and headed next door to Figgerty's. It was pretty quiet in here, just one couple in the front area and a young fellow at the bar. There was a larger area in back with pool tables and a TV.

Being hungry by now, we went back out on the street, walked past the Old Mill, and into the Park Inn. This whole evening has been spent within one block. The Park Inn was fairly crowded, but there was a lot of old dark woodwork and a congenial atmosphere. We found one empty table and got our dinner: Micki had a ham and tomato dish with cheese and chips, and I had an open-faced smoked salmon sandwich. It was all very tasty.

We intended to go back to the Kickham Inn for a little music to top off the night, but as we stepped out the door, it was raining like crazy. This wasn't your usual soft misty Irish rain—it was coming down in sheets. Had we been thinking, we'd have just sat it out. No weather event in Ireland lasts more than fifteen minutes. Instead, we ran down the street toward Fatima House. Micki's Aran sweater was some protection, but I didn't even have a jacket.

About a block away from the B&B we sought shelter in T&M Croke's, a sort of little blue-collar pub. We were soaked to the skin and provided a great deal of amusement to the patrons as we walked in dripping wet. We went over to a table and started to sit down, but the waitress told us, "Don't sit down there. The roof leaks and you'll get wet. Oh, you're already soaked. Here, take that shirt off and I'll get you a dry one." I didn't feel like doing a striptease, so I declined the offer as politely as possible, but she got a little miffed. "Well, I'll at least get you a towel to dry off a bit," she snapped and then went behind the bar and got a big fluffy towel and threw it in my face. The rest of the crowd was enjoying this immensely.

After I'd towelled off some of the water, I felt a chill coming on, and not wishing to succumb to the chills, the plague, the fevers or the ague, I quickly went to the bar and ordered two big Hennesseys as a strictly precautionary measure. The guys sitting at the bar thought that was excellent reasoning and I had a few glasses raised toward me. If I had ordered the cheapest brandy in the house, I'd still have been served Hennessey. It's apparently the general opinion in Ireland that the only brandy worth drinking is Hennessey, and that's usually all that's available.

We dried off a little and let the cognac settle into our systems, and then headed out. Right across the street from Fatima House is the Butler. We went in for a final Hennessey to protect us from any rain-induced illnesses we might contract on the last fifty feet of our night's sojourn. It was pretty crowded and noisy in there. We'd previously noticed some kind of church activity going on up the street, so I figured that an evening of fire and brimstone had worked up a terrible thirst in the faithful, and here they were slaking it away.

We managed to get into the front door of Fatima House without encountering Dick. We were afraid he'd attempt to entertain us with a dozen or so absolutely true stories about drowned rats. We made it undetected to our room and crashed. Although we'd spent almost the entire day in a little rural Irish market town, it had been the most adventurous day yet.

FORTY SHADES OF GREEN

SEPTEMBER 18. After the downpour last night, the day dawned surprisingly clear and bright. Breakfast was at 8:30, and everyone at breakfast was American. There were two young women from California and a couple from Arizona, besides Micki and me. The dining room was very attractive, done up in antiques just like the rest of the house.

Dick served breakfast and then positioned himself in front of the only door to the room. When everybody was served, he started on his stand-up comedy routine. With him in front of the door, nobody could escape; we were stuck until he ran out of air. The breakfast was delicious, though.

The lady from Arizona was a little blabby and somewhat annoying. She stated repeatedly that she didn't like Irish pubs because all people did in them was smoke and drink. I don't know what she expected. After all, a pub is a bar. She did, however, share with us the information that she changed her underwear every day, a fact that everyone was extremely gratified to hear, especially at breakfast.

Dick remarked that Mrs. Arizona reminded him of a young Phyllis Diller, "And I mean that as a compliment. She did have a facelift, didn't she? And what about her husband? Fang, wasn't it? Did he die? Oh, of course not! There he sits." The two California gals were practically choking to keep from laughing. Mr. and Mrs. Arizona didn't seem to know what to do. Maybe they didn't get it.

Part of Dick's routine included an "absolutely true" story about his grandfather building a house with running water. It seems that a stream ran down a hill on his grandfather's property, so he built his house over the stream so that it ran right through the middle of the house. He would take his drinking water from the stream as it entered the house, do his washing slightly downstream in the centre of the house, and you can guess how he used the stream as it left the house. And that's how Dick's grandfather brought indoor plumbing to Ireland. Dick has great taste in dining room stories.

After a few more mouldy old stories that we had heard before, but Dick swore had happened to his grandfather, we managed to escape. It was Monday and we had some business to take care of before we left town.

The town centre is only a few blocks away from Fatima House, so we left Clio and walked. It was a beautiful fall morning, and the short walk was enjoyable. We needed to change money and buy a few necessities. While Micki was shopping in a gift store, I just loitered around on the street, always a pleasant pastime in Ireland. In a few minutes, along came the musician we had chatted with last night at the Kickham Inn. He stopped to bid me good morning and said he missed us last night. I told him that we had intended to show up, but we got caught in the rain and headed home instead. He wasn't offended, but just laughed and said it certainly was a real soaker. He wished me an enjoyable holiday and went on his way up the street.

When Micki came out of the shop, we headed for the *bureau de change* we had passed yesterday where the guy was fixing the door. He was apparently the manager and immediately recognized us and greeted us like we were old friends. We chatted about fixing the door for a little while, just like small town folks would do anywhere. When we inquired about cashing some American travellers' checks, he told us he wouldn't do it because the bank across the street could give us a better rate than he could offer. He would have to cash them himself and be charged a fee for it, which he would have to pass along to us, so it would be cheaper for us if we just went over to the bank and cashed them directly. We thanked him for his help and headed for the bank. I wondered if you would ever find that kind of service in the US.

There are five major banking chains in Ireland; Bank of Ireland and Allied Irish Bank seem to be the biggest. This one in Carrick was an AIB. It was a fairly large establishment and was pretty busy this morning so we had to stand in line and wait our turn (queuing up, as they call it). Since by law or at least custom, all official business is supposed to be bilingual, we were treated to a recorded message in Gaelic every time a teller's window was open. I learned to count and say please while waiting in line.

After leaving the bank, we walked past Pollard's, the pub we had visited yesterday, and there was the same little shaggy dog we had seen then, sitting on the step, letting out pathetic little moans whenever anybody walked by. I guess he was getting impatient for the place to open so he could start his own daily pub-crawl.

When we had finished our business, we headed back to Fatima House to check out and be on our way. We were headed for Cashel, only thirty miles away so we were in no great hurry. After shooing all the neighbourhood cats off Clio, we loaded our luggage and looked for Dick or Nuala to settle up with them. Nuala had already left for her job uptown, but we found Dick in the kitchen. He was reading a pile of postcards that the California ladies had left for him to mail. He said that he probably shouldn't be reading them, and definitely not to us, and then cheerfully proceeded to do just that: "Ireland is a beautiful country. The scenery is gorgeous and the people are very friendly. Some of them are very talkative." Dick's comment: "Isn't that a surprise now?"

We settled our bill and bid our rather long goodbye. It was something like the rural Minnesota ritual in that it extended from the kitchen to the door and out into the driveway and took about fifteen minutes. Dick did say that Nuala had told him that we were very likable guests because we were quiet and didn't act like Americans. I took that for a compliment. We enjoyed his company too. The sharp wit and the leg-pulling stories were thoroughly enjoyable.

It was only about 10:30 when we left Carrick-on-Suir, a little regretfully, I'm afraid. We'd spent less than twenty four hours there, but we'd done so many delightful things with so many lovely people that I'd have liked to stay for awhile. We were now equipped with the Collins atlas and its detailed and complete set of maps, so the prospect of getting lost now was minimized.

It's a fifteen-minute drive on N24 from Carrick-on-Suir to Clonmel, a town that Cromwell had a particular hatred for. From what I'd heard, the locals, both Protestant and Catholic, were not about to let a Puritan Hitler subjugate Clonmel. They put up a hell of a fight, but eventually lost. Cromwell's revenge on the town and its citizens was even more barbaric than his usual methods. He slaughtered most of its citizens and destroyed any building that even suggested Catholicism. When the carnage was done, he set up a garrison to keep things in Tipperary under control. "Cromwellian" is not a nice word in that part of the country.

Clonmel, a good sized market town of 16,000 that looks smaller than it really is, seemed a little easier than most towns to navigate in. The streets are narrow, of course, but are quite a bit straighter than usual. The town is laid out along the River Suir in a long narrow rectangle with the river on the south side and the highway along the north edge. The town seems to be only about six blocks wide. We found a parking place close to the centre of town and set out on foot. Clonmel seemed to be a little more upscale and modern than a lot of rural Irish towns.

Since Micki had by now become a connoisseur of cider and Clonmel is the home of Bulmer's, the most popular Irish cider, we were obligated to make a pub stop for a sample. A half block down the street we ran into the Coachman Bar. It is a little dark place, inhabited mostly by Barry Fitzgerald clones sitting at small tables with a pint of stout and a glass of Paddy in front of each of them. We each got a pint of Bulmer's and sat down. The little old denizens weren't hostile, but they all seemed deep in contemplation about something. Irish memory being what it is, I imagined that they were thinking up satisfying ways of getting back at Cromwell. It's been three and a half centuries, but you can't hurry revenge.

Our thirsts being properly slaked, we headed on down the street. The tourist books said there was a unique Protestant church in town with an impressive octagonal tower. Somewhere in town, there was also supposed to be a town hall dating from the Middle Ages. We decided to check these places out.

After two weeks in Ireland, we had gotten smart enough to go directly to a tourist centre for information. These places are usually full of high school and college kids who will fall all over themselves to help you out.

The Clonmel tourist centre is off the main street about a block toward the river. We got a good street map and some information from a young fellow at the desk. The visit to the town hall was out. We had just walked past it and not recognized it. It was undergoing some massive restoration and repair and was covered with plywood sheets and scaffolding. I thought it was a parking ramp under construction. The hall wouldn't be open to the public for a long while.

We repaired to the Golden Harp back on the main street for another cider and to study the information we had obtained. We found out from the guy at the tourist office that about halfway between Clonmel and Cahir, the next town up the road, was St. Patrick's Well, where the saint is supposed to have baptized the king of Munster. The tourist guy had given us general directions on how to find it, and had offhandedly remarked that it's quite spooky.

We left the Golden Harp and set out to find the church with the octagonal tower. It wasn't far. On the way, we passed a block open to foot traffic only. It was very nicely decorated and lined with various little shops. The Irish being the street people that they are, I imagine that this is a pretty popular place for everyone to hang out.

We found St. Mary's Church (C of I) and wandered around for a bit. The church isn't too ancient, but incorporates part of the medieval city wall in its courtyard. The octagonal tower dates from about two hundred years ago.

After a few pictures, we walked back to the car and then headed out to find St. Patrick's Well. Getting back on N24 was no problem but I couldn't find the turnoff from the highway to the site, so I turned back and got directions again at a petrol station. It turned out that I simply had not gone far enough.

The location of St. Patrick's Well is off the highway about a half-mile on an "other" road. There is a small parking space, a gate in an old stone wall, and beyond that a path leading down about fifty yards into a small wooded hollow. The well is actually a spring that flows out of some rocks into a large pool that in turn empties into a little brook that flows away through the woods. In the centre of the pool is a very weathered Celtic cross dating from the sixth century. The banks of the pool are lined with a rock wall to keep them from caving.

Adjacent to the pool is a small church built in the ninth century. Although roofless, the stone walls are quite sound. I don't know if this place got the treatment from Cromwell, but there are tombs inside the walls dating from the seventeenth century. Carvings on the walls and on the altar are definitely Celtic and must have been put there when the building was first erected.

The guy at the tourist office was right: the place is definitely spooky. Holy wells were an important part of Celtic spirituality long before Christianity arrived on the island. This must have been a holy place long before Patrick's time. Adopting it for Christian purposes was a smart move on his part. The little glen simply reeks mystery. I could well imagine Druids using this place for their ceremonies. The surrounding woods mask out all outside noise, and all that you hear is the flowing water. This definitely qualifies as another thin place.

The water from the spring is reputed to have curative powers so Micki couldn't resist. She went back up to the car and got a plastic mineral water bottle to save some of the spring water in. While she was gone, I sat on a bench and just contemplated antiquity. A couple came down the path and stopped to visit. The guy said he didn't believe that St. Patrick had ever been here, but he didn't sound too convincing, even to himself. After Micki got her bottle of spring water, we left the place feeling a bit subdued, as we usually did after visiting some very ancient place.

We drove through Cahir without stopping and headed north on N8 to Cashel, a distance of only about twelve miles. There's no real problem getting lost in Cashel. The Rock of Cashel is visible for miles and staying oriented with it is pretty easy.

The geography here needs a little explanation. This part of County Tipperary is shaped like a huge flat-bottomed bowl. The Plain of Tipperary, known as the Golden Vale, is very rich farmland surrounded by mountains. From some spots on the edge of the plain, you can see for quite a distance. The constant shift of clouds and sun sends patterns of light across the whole valley. With each shift, the colours change, sometimes subtly, sometimes dramatically, and the various hues of green of the small fields delineated by rock walls are a constantly changing kaleidoscope.

Right in the centre of this bowl, a large granite hill, the Rock of Cashel, juts upward. Because of its strategic location, the Rock has been a stronghold since the Bronze Age. Every ruler of the province of Munster used it as a seat of power right up to the seventeenth century.

The town of Cashel has a population of about 3000 and is very old. There is evidence of the Middle Ages everywhere you look; medieval walls and gateways are incorporated into newer buildings. We headed right for the Rock, paid our admission and started our self-guided tour. Over the many centuries, rulers have added various buildings to the ones that were already there, so you have a very impressive conglomeration of castle, cathedral, service buildings and burial places over the top of the hill. There is a building (or at least the traces) from every century from before the year 1000AD up to the 1600's.

Probably the most awesome structure is the cathedral that sits at the heart of the complex. According to the literature, it is on the site where Brian Boru was crowned High King in 997 AD. The present cathedral was constructed a century or two later. The style is designated "Hiberno-Gothic," which apparently means that it's an Irish variation of the Gothic style being built at the same time on the continent. Although the cathedral is roofless, the rose windows and side chapels are pretty well preserved. Maybe it was just the effect of the open sky, but this seemed to be the largest ancient church we had seen yet, dwarfing even Christchurch and St. Patrick's in Dublin.

Even though there are as many or more religious sites in Ireland as in any other comparable sized area in Europe, the cathedrals and monasteries on the continent are still standing and being used, but in Ireland are mostly in ruins. Irish Catholicism endured over a century of wanton destruction and slaughter at the hands of Henry VIII, Elizabeth I, and the king of butchers, Oliver Cromwell. By the time these gentle rulers got through with their God-given task of destroying Irish Catholicism and its dangerous relative, Irish nationalism, there wasn't much left except a demoralized, landless, leaderless mass of peasants. The Penal Laws of the eighteenth century were simply a codified method of keeping it that way.

Until Cromwell came to Ireland in the 1650's, the Rock of Cashel was a flourishing religious centre and university, rivalling any in Europe. When Cromwell left, there were only damaged walls. And yet, in spite of Cromwell's "divine" mission to destroy Catholicism, Ireland today is the most uniformly Catholic country in Europe. I once heard it said that martyrs for a cause aren't particularly holy, just damned pig-headed. Maybe that's the Irish secret of survival.

After our tour of the Rock, we headed back toward the town centre to get our directions to Ardmayle House, our home for the next two nights. We stopped at Gleeson's Bar for a half-pint and the use of the phone. I called up our hostess, Annette Hunt, and she gave me very specific and clear directions.

We found the place without any difficulty, even though it's located about four miles north east of Cashel on an "other" road. Actually, it was a very scenic little drive. We crossed the River Suir over an old one lane stone bridge and followed the road past a number of beautiful little farms.

I had booked two nights at Ardmayle House months ahead of time, mostly on the enthusiastic review of the place in Frommer's guide. We were not disappointed. The house is a large beautiful stone building set in the middle of a very prosperous farm.

The main house is an ell shaped building with a substantial guest-house beside it, and very old but very tidy outbuildings for the farm around it. All around the place are small lawns and gardens, very well manicured without being fussy. The lane from the road leads up to the main house between small sheep pastures. We were greeted at the door by four goofy but friendly farm dogs. Micki was ecstatic.

For all the appearance of formality and dignity around the place, Annette is an extremely casual lady. She appeared at the door in a faded tail-out flannel shirt and well-worn jeans. She called us both by our first names and told us to make ourselves at home. We were invited to wander around the place anywhere we wanted to. I asked her about fishing, and was told that the Hunts have the fishing rights on the River Suir where it runs through their land, and we were free to "fish to your heart's content."

We checked into our room on the second floor in the 250-year-old part of the house. This one too is all furnished with antiques and has a fireplace that must have been the original. The view out the window is toward the back of the property, overlooking the pasture and the river. Across the river is the ruins of an old medieval tower, and beyond that is the Rock of Cashel in the far distance. It was the most beautiful view we'd had in any of the places we had stayed.

After we had settled in, we went for a walk around the place. We first checked out the river on the backside of the property. The Suir is about 500 yards behind the house, across a pasture. There is a pleasant walkway along the edge of the pasture leading to a bridge. Along the way are holly and ivy growing along an old rock wall that parallels the path. As we were ambling along examining the plant life and occasionally snacking on blackberries, we encountered a bush that had dark blue berries on it and assumed it was a blueberry bush, so we picked a few berries to eat.

Wrong move! The fruit was so bitter that it burned the mouth. We found out later that the bush was a blackthorn and the berries were sloes.

When we got to the river, I was happy to discover that fishing would be easy. The river flows through an open spot and casting from the bank would be fairly simple. I generally lose more flies to bushes and trees than I do to fish. Upriver from the bridge, three big swans were paddling around along the shore. Quite a sight.

We went back toward the house and headed down the lane toward the gate. One of the housedogs, who looked something like a chocolate lab, decided to tag along with us. He was a friendly old mutt and enjoyed walking with us. The lane out to the gate is flanked on both sides by small pastures, interspersed with oak and pine trees. Little flocks of sheep and goats grazed or slept between the trees. It was all very serene and pastoral. The dog more or less guided us on the walk to the gate and back. I guess he does this with anybody who cares for his company.

A little later, when we were about to go back into Cashel for dinner, Annette recommended Hannagan's, located just a few doors away from Gleeson's, where we had used the phone earlier in the afternoon. Finding a good parking spot in Irish towns is generally a crapshoot, but right across the street from Hannagan's is a fair sized parking lot.

Supper was good and hearty. Micki had a serving of lamb medallions and I had the baked breaded cod, served with a bowl of veggies, roasted potatoes, and also french fries. I had asked for tartar sauce with my fish, but didn't get any when it was served. The next time the waitress went by the table, I asked her for it. Quite a while went by, and when she next came in sight, I caught her eye and waved at her. She snapped her fingers and immediately came over with a dish of tartar sauce the size of a soup bowl. She apologized profusely and stated with a huge exaggerated sigh, "But it's a Monday." I guess that explained it.

After we had finished, settled up, and were strolling down the street to the heart of town, the same waitress passed us on the sidewalk with a harried look on her face. She explained that she was heading for the hardware store, because Hannagan's had just run out of cleaning solution. I took it that this was a further explanation about the tartar sauce affair.

Like a lot of Irish towns, Cashel is built on a hillside, so we had to head down hill to get to the town centre. The first pub we stopped at was Feehan's Pub—Funeral Director & Groceries. You'd just have to stop at a place with a name like that. Actually the only part we could see, once we were inside, was the pub. It was another homey likable place with an old look. One jarring note, though, was a row of computer terminals on the back wall for the customers' convenience.

We left Feehan's and crossed the street to Davern's, a place that was supposed to have traditional music. It was a nice place except for the presence of a very Ugly American. He was a guy about forty with small round glasses perched on the end of his nose. There was a boy with him, about 12 or 13, that I assumed was his son. The dad was asking the waitress to bring him small samples of the various beers on tap. He would take each glass, hold it up to the light and examine it, and then take a sip of it and roll it round in his mouth as if it were some vintage wine.

At first, I thought he might be a brewer, at least a home brewer, albeit an obnoxious one, but his comments about the beer revealed that he didn't know beer from cat piss. He was expounding to the kid, the waitress, and anybody else within earshot about how various beers were made, but it was apparent that he knew absolutely nothing about brewing. The poor kid was squirming with embarrassment, but the jackass was oblivious. He seemed to think that beer was made in the same way as Coca-Cola, a "fact" that he repeated several times.

Micki and I were sipping our Paddys and watching all this. It wasn't so much the fact that he was an American moron, (we'd seen plenty of his kind before) but that we were just winding down a glorious day in the Irish countryside, and this jerk was somehow spoiling it. He didn't seem about to knock it off, and I was getting a little hot under the collar. I considered that if I got up and bashed him with a bar stool and the kid called the guard, it would be a safe bet that everyone in the place would agree that the dumb bastard had slipped on a banana peel and that Feehan's—Funeral Director & Groceries was just conveniently across the street.

Micki leaned over to me and asked if I was going to go over and deck him. I said that I was seriously considering it. She said in concerned tone, "Please don't. HE'S MINE!"

Satisfying as it might have been, stomping him into a stain on the floor was not a good idea realistically. We finished our drinks, bid good-bye to the waitress, who waved and gave us a roll of the eyes, and left the place. Traditional music was on Tuesday night anyway.

We made one more pub stop before heading home. A few doors up the street from Davern's is O'Sullivan's. The lady behind the bar was very nice, but she was large and looked as if she would take no crap from any-body. We both wondered what would happen if the "fockin' eejit" from Davern's would come in and start his act. We were half hoping he would. The entertainment would be grand.

It was still early, 9:30, but it had been quite a day. Before we went back to the car, we stopped at a Spar (a franchised convenience store) for some bottled water and an ice cream cone.

When we got back to Ardmayle, we intended to finish writing notes for the day. We went down to the eighteenth century library and sitting room to do so, but it didn't last very long. The fleeting thought struck me that this room was built and furnished about twenty-five years before the Declaration of Independence was written. We both started to nod off while writing, so we called it a day. We'd only travelled 30 miles, but we'd packed in a ton of activity.

THE CHILDREN OF LIR

SEPTEMBER 19. We were up early today for breakfast at 8:00. Today was the day to try my hand at fishing in the River Suir. Annette has quite a reputation as a fly fisher and does conduct guided expeditions. They are quite expensive though and it was pretty late in the season, so I had decided to try it on my own.

At 8:45 I headed down to the river. The sky was clear, but the ground fog was quite thick. I could barely make out the horses in the pasture as I walked down to the river. Micki stayed in the house to rearrange our things and would join me later. When I got to the riverbank, the fog had lifted somewhat, and the sun was shining on the opposite side of river, illuminating the ruined castle in the pasture opposite.

It was incredibly quiet. The sun was bright in the sky, but the ground fog was still fairly dense. The sunlight shining through the fog gave it a pinkish glow. The whole scene had an otherworldly atmosphere.

There is an ancient Celtic legend about King Lir, who loved his four children so intensely that their stepmother was consumed with jealousy. She took the children to a tower on the shores of a lake and put a spell on them, turning them into swans, who were doomed to stay near the tower and lake for nine hundred years.

Immediately after casting the spell, the stepmother was overcome with remorse and tried to retract the curse. She was unable to return the children to their former state, but she was able to give them the gift of beautiful song.

When the nine hundred-year period was over, the children returned to human form, but were ancient and withered. Christianity had come to Ireland by now, and the children were baptized and died a peaceful death. King Lir (who was apparently immortal) decreed that no swan would ever be harmed in Ireland—a law that is still in effect today.

There were wisps of fog floating over the waters of the Suir, and as I was getting my tackle together, eight swans in a perfect line came floating down the river. They made no sound, and I sat very still to keep from breaking the silence. With the castle in the background, and the swans in the pearly fog in the foreground, I definitely felt a thin place again. The swans drifted out of the fog into a small clear space, and then into thicker fog and disappeared down the river. The moment was gone, but I had been there and seen the Children of Lir.

At 9:30 Micki joined me. The fog had pretty much disappeared by this time, and the day was turning beautifully bright and crisp. I wasn't catching anything, but it didn't matter—the experience of being in that place at that time was satisfying enough.

From the river we could see the layout of Ardmayle House more clearly. The original part of the house once faced the river. What is now the back looked like it was formerly the front. That would make sense if the Suir were once a navigable river. At any rate, the view of the house from the river was spectacular. All this time warp kind of thing is disorienting but exhilarating.

I fished and the both of us just hung around on the riverside until about 11:30. I didn't catch anything, but I didn't care. The experience was gratifying anyway.

At noon we went back into town. This time we found a parking place in the heart of town. We stopped for a pint at Dessie's, a very tiny pub on a small side street. We were the only ones there, and the bartender kidded us about Guinness for breakfast. He pulled our pints and drew a shamrock in the foam on the top. I'd heard of this but I thought this was a Boston or Chicago sort of trick. When he served us, he said that with the shamrock on the head of a pint, the beer could be legitimately considered food, since it now contained vegetable matter. I like Irish logic.

The tourist centre was just a few doors away, so we went in and booked a place in Shanagarry, County Cork, for tomorrow night. That done, Micki wanted to do some shopping, so I waited over a pint in Mikey Ryan's Bar, with a few locals who seemed to be doing the exact same thing. The gift shop was next door to Mikey's, so Micki wouldn't have too much trouble finding me. Apparently, the gift shop wasn't too impressive, because Micki walked in just as I was starting to savour my pint. She helped me finish it and we headed out.

At the bottom of the hill, we stopped at the Day-Don Inn. I didn't understand the name, but this is a very old pub. The interior is all stone with a very ancient fireplace built into a sidewall. We ordered our pints and sat at a table near the fireplace to watch the clientele. This seems to be the place for eccentrics to hang out in, so the people watching is pretty enjoyable. Most of the patrons are upwards of eighty or so, and seem to habituate the place.

By now it was 1:45 and we decided to get some lunch. We went back to Feehan's (Funeral etc.) and got in on the tail of the lunch crowd. I had a ploughman's lunch, which is a cold plate of ham, cheese and onion slices, and washed it down with a pint of Smithwick's Ale. (If you're ever going to order this ale, pronounce it "Smiddick," as the locals do.)

Cashel is getting famous worldwide for their farmhouse cheeses, the best of which, in my opinion, is Cashel Blue. After lunch, we went on a search mission for some of it. We had seen some at the tourist centre previously, but when we checked with them, they were out and hadn't gotten their ration for the day yet. They suggested we try the grocery stores across the street. We checked at the Super Value store, but they only had large wheels that they didn't want to cut.

We headed for the Spar store, but got sidetracked at Cantrell's, a small, attractive pub on the way. We had an after-lunch settler here, and admired all the leaded glasswork in the place.

When we got to the Spar, we found out the same story: they didn't want to cut a large wheel of cheese. Instead, we bought a bag of pinhead oatmeal to take home and make brown bread with.

Since it was still early, we went back to Ardmayle House to rest a bit before supper. We sat out on a bench in the back and made notes for the day. Although we were in the shadow of the house, we could see the Rock of Cashel in full sunlight in the distance. Knowing that we'd be leaving all this behind tomorrow, we just sat and absorbed as much as we could.

At 7:00 we returned to town for supper. We stopped in for a pre-dinner drink at Dowling's Bar. This was a very tidy little place with gorgeous leaded glass windows and a stone fireplace in the lounge area. It was a good place to begin the evening.

While walking around earlier in the day, we had noticed Bailey's Restaurant and had studied the menu posted outside. We decided to have dinner there. It was a rather small place with the dining room down a few steps below street level. There weren't many people in the place, and when we asked for a table for two, the waitress obligingly moved some tables around so that we could have a small table with a little privacy.

There was a group of six Americans across the room from us who caught our attention because, although they were enjoying themselves thoroughly, they were quiet and mannerly. They complimented the waitress on the decor, her service and the food. It was a rare great relief to see Americans behaving themselves.

For our meal, we each had a different preparation of chicken. Micki had roast chicken with a cream sauce chock full of Cashel Blue cheese. I had what they called Gaelic Chicken, which was basically the same thing as Micki's, except that the sauce was a very rich concoction of Irish whiskey and wild mushrooms. This was all accompanied by a serving of fresh hot-buttered carrots and real mashed potatoes. It was incredibly good, but it was also a reminder that we hadn't yet purchased any Cashel Blue to take home. We'd have to find some before we left town.

Bailey's is at the bottom of the long hill that forms Cashel's main street. We headed back up hill and stopped for a second visit at Davern's. We looked around apprehensively to see if the Fockin' Eejit (our permanent name for last night's beer connoisseur) was in attendance. He wasn't anywhere to be seen. Micki's theory was that somebody did the world a favour and stuffed him head first through the bung and into an empty Guinness barrel in the back alley.

At any rate, we sat at the bar and ordered a Paddy each. The young girl tending bar greeted us like we were old friends, remarking that she had seen us here last night and that she particularly remembered us because she had gotten mad at the barman who waited on us when he served our drinks in ugly glasses. She was glad we had come back so she could serve us with some better looking ones. A glass is pretty much a glass to me, but I was glad to see that she felt she'd set things right. We chatted for a while with this pleasant little lady, but she never mentioned the obnoxious beer sampler. If Micki's theory was correct and she had had a hand in his disappearance, it was better not to find out.

We decided to make one more pub stop before we left Cashel for good. We walked to the top of the hill and turned right on a street we hadn't been on before. About a half block away there was a sign indicating Billy Foley's Pub, and we headed for it. Just short of Foley's, there was a very tiny convenience store. We went in and checked it out, and they had Cashel Blue in the size we wanted. We bought what we needed and headed out well satisfied.

Billy Foley's was decent but undistinguished. Most pubs are very quiet compared with American bars, unless there is a significant sporting event on TV. Then they can get pretty noisy. That was the case in Billy Foley's. There was some sort of semi-final going on, and the regulars would let out a cheer or a boo whenever the occasion called for it. They weren't rude or obnoxious, just enthusiastic.

Full and sleepy by this time, we headed back to Ardmayle House. As we got out into the country, we could occasionally see the Rock of Cashel lit up by floodlights. Quite a sight. I think I'm going to miss this place.

BALLYMALOE

SEPTEMBER 20. We were up in time for breakfast at 8:00 AM. The dining room at Ardmayle House is in the "new" section of the house. This part is a mere century old. The dining room has a modern glassed-in sunroom opening out onto the courtyard, so guests can watch the Hunts starting out their daily business of running the farm. The morning was crisp and bright, and it was pleasant watching the dogs heading out to the paddocks to tend the sheep. It was like a short scene from a Technicolor movie from the Fifties.

After breakfast, we said goodbye to the Hunts and thanked them profusely for their hospitality. When we told Annette how much we enjoyed their beautiful place, she said that they had opened as a B&B mostly as a way to put a lot of empty space to use. The farm has been in the family for 140 years and age has only added to the grandeur of the place. I wish the Hunts at least another century of good fortune.

By 9:30 we were headed back to Cashel. We stopped in the centre of town and took care of two matters: sending my fly rods home and getting a place to stay for Thursday night.

Sending off the fly rods was a simple matter. The clerk at the post office (*Oifig an Phoist* officially) asked if I was in a hurry to get the rods home. This should have been a warning bell, but I missed it. I told him there was no big rush, so we sent them off at the cheapest rate. Two months later they arrived home. I should have known by now that the Irish measure speed by a very different standard.

Getting a place to stay was no problem either. The tourist office is only a few doors away from the Post Office, so we dropped in and inquired about a place in Dingle, County Kerry, our destination for Thursday night. Within a few minutes, we had a place booked and were on our way.

We now headed south from Cashel toward County Cork. This was going to be one of the big events of the trip. A few days earlier I had made reservations for dinner tonight in Shanagarry, County Cork, at Ballymaloe House, a very prestigious restaurant, and we were eagerly looking forward to it.

We took N8 south to Cahir and then southeast through Mitchelstown and on to Fermoy, where we gassed up. A few miles past Fermoy we stopped for a stretch and a pint at Barry's Bar in Rathcormac, a little village with only three pubs. The main decor in Barry's is a smoke-darkened ceiling covered with souvenir matchbooks. The chatty lady behind the bar told us with a straight face not to ask for matches; there aren't any.

Micki asked where the ladies' room was and was directed around the corner to another bar and dining area. To get there, she had to duck through an opening under the bar ("Mind your head now!"). No explanation, no apologies or excuses: that's just how you get to the toilet in here.

The lady (I assumed that she was the owner) told us that she had a son who was working on a threshing crew in the States. He started his season in North Dakota and was presently in Kansas. I think this was the first time we talked to anyone with a relative in the US somewhere besides Boston or New York.

We left Rathcormac at about 12:30 PM and headed south again. Marie, our hostess for this evening, had told us to follow R626 from Rathcormac to Midleton, where we could pick up the road to Shanagarry. We decided against it. With the Collins Road Atlas, we weren't afraid of getting lost anymore. Instead we followed N8 to where it joins N25 just east of Cork City. We turned east on N25, which is a dual carriageway, and proceeded to Midleton. It may have been slightly longer in miles, but it certainly was a much better road.

We had to stop at Midleton Distillery. Not that we are fond of Irish whiskey (Ha!), but that is where the local tourist office is located. Loath as we might have been, there was no way of avoiding the distillery.

Practically all Irish whiskey production is controlled by an umbrella group—Irish Distillers. This includes all the familiar labels (Bushmill's, Jameson, Midleton) and a number that aren't available in the US. I'm not familiar with all the intricacies of international conglomerates, but I think that the Irish Distillers is basically a marketing group that promotes Irish whiskey throughout the world. My personal opinion is that it doesn't need much promoting—one taste and you're an enthusiast.

Through the Gulliver system, we made bookings at the tourist office for our last two nights of the trip. We had intended to find a place in Listowel, as recommended by Eamon, the bartended in Ballina. However, Listowel is a centre for horse racing, there was going to be a race meet on the upcoming weekend, and there wasn't a room to be had. We booked a place in Abbeyfeale instead. Saturday night, our last, we would be staying at Bunratty Villa, not far from the airport.

After all that was taken care of, we were seized with a powerful thirst, and being about fifty feet from a distillery and its tasting room, we thought it would be extremely rude to pass up any hospitality available.

Midleton's tasting room is a little more formal than Bushmill's. It also charges for samples. I tried a Jameson Reserve, and Micki sampled Redbreast, a brand I'd never seen in the US. Both were very good. Irish whiskey doesn't need promotion, just an introduction.

Shanagarry is a very short distance from Midleton, and the signs leading to Shanagarry Bed and Breakfast were quite clear. The B&B is located about a half mile from Darina Allen's Ballymaloe Gardens and Cooking School.

Our interest in Ballymaloe started one Christmas when my daughter Santina gave me *The Complete Book of Irish Country Cooking* by Darina Allen. The book is a gem full of basic recipes interspersed with stories about Irish food and rural living in the past. We were quite impressed with the book, and after seeing Darina on TV, we decided that a trip to Ireland must include dinner at Ballymaloe.

The author also mentions her husband's parents, Myrtle and Ivan Allen, quite frequently. Sometime ago, in the late forties, I think, young Ivan and Myrtle scrimped and mortgaged and borrowed enough money to purchase a large farm in the Cork countryside outside Shanagarry. The intent at first was to simply farm, but Myrtle began serving meals and the place got a reputation for extremely high quality. Over the years, the business expanded into a very popular guesthouse.

Darina Allen began as an employee at Ballymaloe House and eventually married Tim Allen (no, not the Home Improvement guy), Myrtle and Ivan's oldest son. As Ballymaloe House grew, the younger Allens took over an old farm several miles away and opened up Ballymaloe Gardens and Cooking School. Darina gradually earned a well-deserved reputation as a cooking instructor, cookbook author, and television personality. The emphasis at the whole Ballymaloe enterprise is freshness and high quality ingredients, served with a gracious informality, and because of that, the place has become one of the most prestigious places in Europe, without being snobbish. Once, when Ivan was asked what all the Allens did at Ballymaloe, he thought for a moment and then replied with the understatement of the century, "Well, we raise sheep."

We had our personal experience with Ballymaloe House informality when I booked dinner reservations several days earlier. The lady on the phone asked for my name and when I told her, she remarked, "Oh, what a lovely name!" I asked her if a jacket and tie were required for dinner, and she answered, "Oh, no. Just dress comfortably, but please, Mr. Lovelace, no raggedy jeans, OK?"

We found Shanagarry Bed & Breakfast without any difficulty. It was only 3:45, so we had plenty of time on our hands before our dinnertime at 7:00. Marie, our hostess, suggested we look over Ballycotton Harbour, only about two miles away. She gave us very clear directions and I was beginning to wonder if we were starting to go native, since instructions seemed to make more sense everyday. Not an unpleasant thought.

Ballycotton is a picturesque little village where Ballymaloe House gets its seafood daily. The restaurant staff goes down to the harbour and picks the fish right off the boat. Everything served in the evening was caught that day.

We parked "up in the town" as the Irish say, and wandered down to the beach. The tide was out and there were little pools here and there with shellfish attached to the still wet rocks. Had we known what these creatures were, we could have picked a few, and helped out a guy down the shore collecting them from the rocks. We selected a comfortable boulder with some natural seats on it and lunched on the brown bread and Cashel Blue and Gubbeen cheese we had brought along. There wasn't a cloud in the sky at the moment, and the view up the coast was superb. There is a lighthouse on an island at the mouth of the harbour, and at low tide, it appeared that you could walk out to it. It was the most scenic lunch anyone could ask for.

After wandering around on the shore for awhile, we headed back up to the street and turned into Lynch's Inn by the Harbour. The place was small and very much a local hangout. It was the first pub we visited where we didn't get the usual friendly welcome. Nobody was rude, but the conversation among the few locals stopped when we walked in the door. It seemed as if we were walking into some kind of private club. We ordered our half-pints (Beamish Stout this time, since we were in County Cork), finished them off quickly and quietly, and left.

We still had some time available, so we drove back to Shanagarry and turned in at Ballymaloe Gardens and Cooking School, which turned out to be only about 100 yards up the road from our B&B. The restaurant and gift shop were closed for the day, but we were given a map and were told to feel free to walk around on our own. Normally there is a charge for tours of the place, but the young lady at the counter just said, "Och, forget about it. Just go ahead." Our temporarily bruised appreciation for Irish hospitality was immediately restored.

All the old buildings of the one-time farm have been restored and put to use as dormitories, classrooms, and demonstration kitchens for the school. The Allens have managed to accomplish all this without losing the atmosphere of an old estate. It is, of course, still a working farm with emphasis on free-range livestock and chemical free produce. In addition, there are extensive formal classical gardens, probably used as landscape demonstrations.

We strolled around for about an hour, just admiring the industry and ingenuity it must have taken to get all this so well organized without being fussy or stuffy. Our one small disappointment was not getting to see Darina Allen. This would have been a great moment in our ongoing collection of Irish celebrities.

After we left the gardens, we went back to the B&B to get ready for the big event of the week: dinner at Ballymaloe House. It was a very short drive of three miles to the place. The driveway into the complex presents quite a view. The house itself is several hundred years old and looks a lot like Ardmayle House, but was built about a century earlier. Ballymaloe House is a bit more upscale and extensive than Ardmayle, with tennis courts, a swimming pool and several gift shops that feature the work of local artists and craftsmen. These are not the usual souvenir shops with plastic tourist junk; the products are high quality original pottery, textiles, and paintings.

It was a bit after 7:00, but nobody seemed to mind. Surprisingly, we weren't concerned either. I guess Irish timing was starting to rub off on us. We were escorted to a comfortable small wing off the main dining room to a table with a hand-lettered placard on it reading "Reserved for Mr. and Mrs. Lovelace." We were a little nervous about being here hob-nobbing with the very wealthy, but we needn't have worried. Every guest is treated here with such easy gracious informality that we soon felt very much at home.

A very nice middle-aged lady, who was quite conversational without being obnoxious, served us. It was a treat to be addressed politely and quietly by a dignified mature lady, who would never give out the usual annoying American waitress greeting of "Hi, Ya Guys!! How are YOU? Graaate!!" When we told the server that this was our belated anniversary dinner (thirty-second to be precise), she congratulated us and wished us many more.

The menu at Ballymaloe House changes nightly, in keeping with the Allens' philosophy that fresh food is the best food. The dinner consists of five courses, with several choices for each course. For the first course, we both had the fresh mushroom soup—a delightful concoction of pureed mushrooms and cream.

For the second course, Micki had the gourgettes (squash blossoms) stuffed with goat cheese and basil, served with tomatoes and olives. I had the Danish pâté, served with large croutons.

For the third and main course, Micki had the lamb roast with corian-der served over a pureed squash. I had baked haddock with chili garlic and herbed butter surrounded by scarlet runner beans. Vegetables served with both entrees were sautéed red and yellow peppers, potatoes, and Brussels sprouts.

The fourth course was a sort of palate cleanser. The waitress rolled a cart up to the table, and displayed on its top were about a dozen varieties of cheese. These weren't just little nibbles; they were large quarter and half wheels. When the waitress asked us what we wanted to try, I sam-pled two different kinds of Irish farmhouse cheese, and Micki had an Irish Camembert and a variety of goat cheese. The tangy earthy taste was an excellent complement to the substantial main course.

For the dessert course, I had a dish of incredibly rich caramel ice cream covered (get this) with a *caramel sauce*! Micki was more restrained: she had a fragrant lemon torte. We finished off our feast with coffee and Courvoisier.

I had been prepared for an extremely expensive dinner, but the total came to a little over £70, about $80. I've spent much more for a mediocre meal in the US.

We left Ballymaloe in a state of stuffed euphoria. It was beginning to get a little blustery outside, but we made it back to Shanagarry B&B before it began to rain. We had accomplished another goal, and wouldn't soon forget Ballymaloe.

BRENDAN'S COUNTRY

SEPTEMBER 21. It had rained pretty hard during the night, but we hadn't heard a thing. Rain comes down pretty quietly in Ireland, even when it's heavy, not at all like Minnesota thunderstorms that usually consist of hail, strong winds and lots of lightning. When we came down to breakfast, the rain had stopped, but the ground was still quite wet.

We sat at a table with a lady from Northern Ireland who runs a guesthouse in Armagh and was here in Shanagarry observing at Ballymaloe Gardens, learning about organic gardening. Because it was so wet, she had decided not to go to the Gardens today. Over a delicious breakfast of smoked salmon and scrambled eggs, she urged us to spend more time in the north on our next visit in order to soak up the history. She was well aware that many Americans are apprehensive about visiting Northern Ireland, and was trying to tell us that it is still worth visiting. I heartily concur. I noticed that she said "when" we return, not "if," an assumption I liked to hear.

We left Shanagarry at 9:15 and headed back to N25. This road heads directly for Cork City, but fortunately there is a wide well marked bypass around the south side of the city, and even though the morning traffic was heavy, we got past Cork without any trouble.

We headed west from Cork on N22 and arrived in Ballymakeery at 11:10. It's a very pretty little town, and we immediately noticed that we were again in the Gaeltacht—many signs were posted in Gaelic only. O'Scanaill's Bar in Ballymakeery is a bright yellow building that got our attention immediately. We stopped in for a pit stop, a stretch, and a half-pint. The very friendly young girl behind the bar drew us our pints and then leaned her chin on the beer taps and proceeded to fill us in on what was going on in rural County Kerry. We talked about the weather, the roads and especially about the upcoming All-Ireland finals in Gaelic football. Kerry and Galway were the finalists in a match scheduled for Sunday September 24. She told us to watch for all the green and gold banners we'd see from here all through County Kerry. She also gave us the inside scoop: Galway was sure to win. As we left, Micki remarked that we were not going to mention anything about Galway while we were in Kerry. She figured that the Irish have had enough revolts and rioting, and given their passion for sports, it was not up to us to instigate any more.

We left Ballymakeery and followed N22 to Killarney. We would have liked to visit here, and we bypassed the city reluctantly, but we weren't too sure what the roads would be like ahead. We crossed the Slieve Mish Mountains and joined N21 just outside of Tralee. The scenery was getting more rugged and majestic with every mile. We picked up N86 at Tralee and came within sight of the Atlantic. We were now on the north side of the Dingle Peninsula, and realized that we had made better time than we imagined. We were only about 20 miles from Dingle Town.

We stopped at the small village of Camp for a stretch and some pictures. The Junction Bar had a fairly roomy parking lot (about ten spaces), and a gorgeous view of Tralee Bay out its back. We went out on the back deck and soaked up the view. For a small country, Ireland sometimes gives the impression of vast spaces.

From our vantage point behind the pub, we could see the expanse of the bay, dotted with fishing boats at work, and sailboats out for a day's cruise. The hillside that ran down to the shore below us was divided into small fields by the ever-present rock walls. Inside each field was a collection of sheep and cattle grazing on the rich grass. Distances in Ireland can be tricky to judge visually, so I'd be hard pressed to say exactly how far we could see, but the scene seemed to be infinite.

After enjoying a half-pint and the atmosphere of the Junction, we headed on our way. Just outside of Camp, the road turns and crosses the mountains to the south side of the Dingle peninsula. It didn't look too far to Dingle Town on the map, but the map didn't say anything about how fast you could go. We were on a national highway, but it had so many hairpins in it that 20 mph was an impossible speed. Fortunately, what little traffic there was moved at a cautious and sensible rate.

There was a layby before we reached the top of the mountains, and we stopped for a few pictures. The light that day was constantly shifting, and the colours of the fields, mountains and ocean shifted accordingly. You might snap a picture, wait ten seconds, snap the same scene but get an entirely different effect.

We crossed the spine of the mountains and began descending toward the south side of the Dingle Peninsula. There was another layby with a great view of Dingle Bay and the Iveragh Peninsula in the distance across the bay. We took a few pictures and then headed toward Dingle.

The Dingle Peninsula is unusually rich in ruins and remains dating back to the early Christian era in Ireland. Probably one of the most colourful and famous tales of that time is the voyage of St. Brendan the Navigator. Brendan was born sometime in the late fifth century AD near Tralee and became a monk. Harsh penances were a part of monastic life in those days, and the penance considered the most severe was going into voluntary exile. According to his own account, Brendan, accompanied by seventeen other monks, set sail into the Atlantic in a small curragh from the mouth of Brandon Creek on the Dingle Peninsula.

The written report of Brendan's voyage, the *Navigatio*, is really an allegory depicting a spiritual journey rather than a physical one. However, there are very detailed descriptions of various places the sailor/monk visited, which has led scholars ever since to speculate on the location of these places. Some historians claim that Brendan actually reached the North American continent.

There is some evidence that points to that possibility. It has been proven that Irish monks (known as Culdees) did sail as far as Iceland in the seventh and eight centuries. There are mysterious buildings still standing in New England and Virginia that bear a striking resemblance to the beehive cells common to monasteries in Ireland in Brendan's time. Moreover, near the buildings in Virginia are rocks inscribed with what some experts claim is the old Irish alphabet, known today as *Ogham*.

There is no direct proof that Brendan sailed to North America, but the vague hints are tantalizing. Early explorers, such as Leif Erickson and Columbus himself, were familiar with Brendan's account. In 1976, Tim Severin and a few friends built a replica of a sixth century curragh, sailed it from Brandon Creek, and after several months arrived in Newfoundland. The voyage didn't prove that Brendan sailed to the New World, but it did prove that it was possible.

If I had to make a list of the most attractive places in Ireland, Dingle would be in the top three. It's a very old village with a reputation of extreme independence. In fact, at one time, the inhabitants declared themselves an independent country and began minting their own money. Apparently this didn't last very long, but it gives a good indication of the local attitudes. Dingle also has a long tradition of being the smuggling capital of Ireland. That's not too surprising, considering its isolated location and the close-knit character of its people.

Today, Dingle is a small but prosperous fishing town that has capitalized on the tourist boom. The town has become one of the really hot tourist spots in Europe, without sacrificing its unique character. This is no Gaelic-speaking Disneyland. Tourists are welcome and treated well, but there is no artificial attempt to commercialise the place. The locals carry on their lives pretty much as they always have, and visitors are welcome to join in, but if one doesn't like it, the road also goes back inland, don't you know.

Dingle's streets are really narrow, but by now, we had gotten used to narrow Irish streets and pretty much taken them for granted. On arriving in town, we headed for the very modern and efficient tourist office right on Dingle Harbour. There was ample parking, with only a few tour buses. It was only 2:00 PM, so we had plenty of time to do some strolling. We took a few minutes to look over the harbour, and were pretty impressed with what nature had created. The harbour is not particularly big, but it is well protected from the ocean. There is a very narrow neck at its entrance and then it widens into a small bay surrounded by fairly high hills. I would imagine that it's pretty secure against strong storms.

We headed up the street away from the harbour and stopped at a pub, Maire De Barra. The lunch crowd was still there, and it was pretty busy. We had a half-pint and went back out on the street. Being in a fishing town, we felt a very serious obligation to have some fish and chips. There was a "chipper" just a few doors down from the pub, so we took advantage. In spite of all the old traditional atmosphere in Dingle, the interior of the shop looked pretty much like every other fast food place in the world. We placed our order at the counter, just like at McDonald's, and waited for them to prepare it. Very shortly, it was ready, but at this point we got snapped back to Ireland. Micki had ordered the cod and chips, and I had gotten the smoked haddock and chips. What we each got was a huge slab of deep fried fish, still sizzling, and a tremendous serving of french fries. Fast food may have invaded Ireland, but skimpy portions haven't, thanks be to God. Seasoned with plenty of salt and malt vinegar, the meal was delicious. Dinner would have to be later in the evening tonight; lunch was going to stick with us for awhile.

We realized by now that Dingle had a lot to offer, and that we had better start exploring to find out how we could best spend the evening. It was starting to sprinkle a bit so we took a very short detour back to the car to get jackets and umbrellas, and then headed back down the street and stopped into Paudie's Bar to check it out. It was pretty quiet in here, nothing too extraordinary, but they had a sign advertising traditional music later in the evening, something to consider.

It's pretty hard to tell what's a main street in Dingle. There are no square corners, and streets run in all directions and all angles. We headed up a street to do a little window-shopping and menu reading. Micki had decided that Dingle was the place to fulfill a solemn, almost religious, obligation to have a whole fresh lobster. We could not go back home without doing this. We found a place, Fenton's, that had lobster on the menu for the evening, so that was going to be our dinner spot.

We wandered around a bit more, and I'm glad we did. We found *Ua Flaibeartaig* (O'Flaherty's), a very old traditional pub. We dropped in for a half-pint, looked around and decided that this was going to be the place for tonight's music. O'Flaherty's is about 200 years old and the Gaelic was floating all over the place. This was it.

With all the essentials for the evening decided now, (dinner, drinks and music), we started back downhill for the car. The fine day (light rain) had turned into a fine soft day (heavy rain). When we turned the corner at the bottom of the hill, the wind hit us and turned umbrellas useless. The rain was coming nearly horizontally off the ocean, the umbrellas turned inside out, and we got soaked. We stopped into a few shops on the way, and eventually got back to the car, at which point the rain stopped, and the sun came out.

We had directions to our B&B, and we had no trouble finding it. Dingle is surprisingly small, so getting lost isn't a major disaster. At any rate, Dingle Heights B&B was a lucky choice. It sits on the hill behind the town with a gorgeous view of the harbour. We could also get a picture of the layout of Dingle from here.

Yet another Fitzgerald family runs Dingle Heights. A pleasant little rosy-cheeked lady greeted us at the door and then cheerfully showed us to our room upstairs. On the way up there was a schedule of Mass times posted on the wall. In nearly three weeks in Ireland, that was the first time we'd seen that.

After towelling off the Dingle rain and taking a bit of a rest, and watching the ever-present cow pasture in the back of the house, we started in for town. Dingle being as small as it is, we chose to walk. The road in front of Dingle Heights heads right into the town centre, past the community hospital, which is big enough for a useful landmark. From the outside, the hospital looked about as old as anything else in town. It looked pretty quiet—few cars in the parking lot, and no ambulance sirens.

When we got to Fenton's, we were seated at a table for two and, as seems customary in Irish restaurants, all the tables were quite close together. We had gotten used to this by now, accepting the fact that personal space in Ireland is different than in the US.

Micki's quest for a whole live lobster was about to commence. About four feet away was a glass tank full of live, and lively, lobsters. You just knew these critters had been frisking around at the bottom of the Atlantic just a few hours ago. The price of lobster was determined by weight, so a diner just pointed out a specimen in the tank and the waitress would tell you what the price was. When Micki picked out her choice and I mentally calculated what this meal would cost, I was tempted to tell the waitress I'd just have one sardine and a glass of water. However, I restrained myself. The Irish are supposed to be the comedians, and tourists are the straight men.

When it was time to order, I requested a dish of steak medallions in Cashel Blue sauce, a delicious, but rather tame order as things turned out. The waitress reached into the tank up to her shoulder and grabbed Micki's lobster. This one must have been the meanest crustacean that ever crawled Dingle Bay. I swear I could hear him screaming Gaelic curses. He wasn't going to his doom meekly. As soon as the waitress got him out of the tank, he took a couple of swipes at her with his claws, and started twisting and flailing. The waitress dropped him, and as soon as he hit the floor, he made a beeline for the exit. She caught him before he could escape and carted him off to the kitchen. All the other lobsters were lined up in the tank watching. I think they were laughing. The victim may have been a bully and they were happy to see justice done.

Of course, all this commotion attracted the attention of the other diners. From now on, they kept an eye on us to see how this was going to turn out. In due course, our dinners arrived. Micki's lobster was pretty subdued by now, having been boiled and cut into pieces. Micki took one look at her plate and decided that there was no way to eat this elegantly. The only thing to do was to go at it with both hands, and she did, much to the amusement of the other diners. But who cared? You don't eat like this very often.

We left Fenton's well satisfied with the food and the drama. We set out for O'Flaherty's for the music, which wouldn't start for another hour and a half or so, but arriving early guarantees a good seat. It wasn't crowded when we got there, so we found a good corner table not far from where the musicians would be playing. We ordered our pints and settled in for some people watching.

There were some young people sitting at a nearby table to our right. They were mostly young guys in their twenties, but there was a young man and wife from New York in the group. He was asking about Irish sports, and the other guys were filling him in, probably with a good deal of exaggeration. The New Yorker said he didn't have a clue about anything and he just wanted to learn a few things. This wasn't too remarkable, except that it was a rarity to see a young American being civil and enjoying his experience.

The group broke up after a while, and the young New Yorkers left. One of the guys in the group came over and sat beside me. He was from Germany and spends his vacation every year travelling. He'd been to Ireland several times in the last couple of years. His method is to stay in youth hostels and ride around on buses to wherever the spirit moves him. He was quite talkative and his English was flawless. He was pretty interesting to pass the time with.

The music started at 9:30. The group tonight consisted of two guys, one of whom I had seen in here earlier in the day. He seemed to be the owner or manager. Frommer's guide noted that the present owner, Fergus O'Flaherty, often sings in the evening, so this may have been Fergus himself. The other musician was a guy that could have been a stand-in for Spencer Tracy. He had thick white hair and a weathered face that just looked Irish. The two played and sang for about two and a half hours. It was tremendous! A lot of it was familiar, but a good deal of it was new to me. Quite a few songs were in Gaelic; some were sung without musical accompaniment. The white haired guy played an accordion and sang, while his partner played a guitar, flute, penny whistle and sang. It was all very natural and without pretence or showmanship. They finished off the session with the very haunting "Cliffs of Doneen," and the crowd was very appreciative.

While the music was going on, a man and woman, perhaps in their middle sixties, had sat down at our table. After a while, the man said something to her, and then left. The woman, who couldn't have weighed more than 90 lbs., turned to start talking to us during one of the musicians' breaks. She said she was originally from Cork, but now she lived in England. It sounded as if she and her husband (who had just left) manage a golf course; he takes care of the grounds, and she does the cooking at the clubhouse. She said she couldn't stand to eat breakfast anymore because she cooks so many of them. She also told us that her maiden name was Ireland; she was a Miss Ireland before there were any contests for the title. Her husband had left because he was tired, but he was supposed to come back and get her later.

After all this, the musicians were done and starting to pack up. I went up to the Spencer Tracy look-alike and in very elementary Gaelic thanked him and told him the music was great. He shook my hand and likewise in Gaelic thanked us for coming and wished us a safe journey. I never thought in my younger days that I would ever be chatting with a Kerryman in Dingle in his own language.

When we left O'Flaherty's, the weather had cleared and we had an invigorating moonlit walk home. Tired but exhilarated, we reached Dingle Heights and retired. Once again, the *craic* had indeed been mighty.

MORE FITZGERALDS

SEPTEMBER 22. The sky was slightly overcast when we went down to breakfast at 8:30. The dining room at Dingle Heights is at the front of the house in a sort of glassed in porch. The view was tremendous from where we were seated. We could see the entire harbour and the fishing fleet going out to sea one boat at a time through the neck of the harbour. In the far distance, across Dingle Bay, we could see the mountains of the Iveragh Peninsula, where the well-known Ring of Kerry is located.

Chatting with the staff, who seemed to be having a great deal of fun, we found out that the cheery lady wasn't Mrs. Fitzgerald the owner, but a lady that came in occasionally to help run the place. Mrs. Fitzgerald was out of town for a few days, and it felt like this was a "when the cat's away" situation going on. I guessed that Mrs. Fitzgerald usually runs a pretty tight ship. However, the staff was doing an excellent job keeping everyone satisfied. Mrs. Fitzgerald left the place in good hands.

By 9:30 we were packed and ready to head out. We planned to spend the morning in town doing a little shopping and strolling. We settled up with the ladies and they wished us "*Slán abhaile*" (A safe journey home).

As it was still early in the day, there were plenty of parking spaces available in town . Being the tourist centre that it is, there are craft and gift shops all over the place, most carrying high quality merchandise. We had gotten so self-confident by now that we split up, Micki heading for some shops and me just wandering around. We agreed to meet in front of the bank a little later. I just strolled around and occasionally stood on a corner chatting with whoever came by. I did run into the cheery little lady from the B&B. I wished her good morning (for the second time that day) and she replied with a grin that we'd have to stop meeting like this.

Micki and I finally connected, and we decided to try a couple of pubs before we left. Dingle reputedly is home to fifty-two pubs, and we hadn't even scratched the surface. We stepped into *An Droighead Beag* (The Little Bridge). I didn't catch the significance of the name, as there didn't seem to be a bridge anywhere near. We had our half-pints while the Guinness deliveryman exchanged the empty kegs from the night before for full ones for today. A couple of guards walked in and headed toward the back. Apparently they were in for an early lunch.

We left and headed down the street a few doors to the Dingle Pub. I'd seen pictures of this place in books on Ireland, and we simply couldn't leave Dingle without a visit there. It was a bit bigger than most pubs, but had a lot of attractive woodwork and had a very comfortable feel to it.

By now it was pretty close to noon and we felt that we had better be on our way. On the way back to the car, just down the street from *An Droighead Beag,* we noticed a very interesting house. A small stream ran down the hill parallel to the street, and this house was built on a bridge over the stream. The Little Bridge now made sense. I recalled Dick Gaul's story about his grandfather's house built over a stream. We thought it was just one of his entertaining stories, but apparently this was done occasionally, and here was the evidence right in front of us. It made me wonder how many of Dick's "absolutely true" stories actually were.

We left Dingle with a great deal of regret. Had we known what a great place it was, we would have scheduled more time there. There are a lot of pubs that we need to visit, and we made a firm intention to return in the future.

We started back on N86 the way we had come. Actually we had no choice—there's only one road into Dingle. We turned off N86 at Anascaul to take the coast road R561. We had skipped the Ring of Kerry, a spectacular scenic drive across the bay, but we figured that this would be a reasonable substitute. We were right. A few miles down the road is

Inch Strand, a very long sandy point that juts out into Dingle Bay at a nearly perfect right angle. Micki is fascinated with surf, and there was certainly plenty of it at Inch. We pulled into a car park, posted with a list of restrictions concerning the beach—no dogs without a leash, no driving on the beach, no camping except in designated areas. From the looks of it, everyone completely ignores the rules.

The day had cleared off by now, and it was quite warm on the beach. There were a few windsurfers trying their luck, but they didn't seem to be having much success getting out past the breakers. The waves looked pretty ferocious and the wind was fairly strong. The water looked frigid.

Micki was in seventh heaven. Quote: "The roar of the sea—how awesome! There is something about the sound, eerie and speaks with authority." She was certainly on the mark here. The rhythmic boom and roar as each wave broke can certainly shrink any arrogance a puny human being might have.

We wandered around the beach for about an hour. Being landlocked flatlanders from the middle of a continent, we poked around at everything we saw: seaweed, shells, rocks and pools. We picked up some shells to take back to the grandkids and just puttered around. A fellow came down to the beach with two beautiful border collies (no leash). He'd toss a stick and they'd tear after it, just having the greatest time.

Before we left, we stopped at the little visitor centre near the parking lot. Some scenes from the movie *Ryan's Daughter* were filmed on Inch Strand, so we picked up some literature on the movie to peruse on the plane trip home.

After leaving Inch, we continued up R561 to Castlemaine. This is a regional road, and rather narrow, but the scenery was spectacular and we were really not in too big a hurry; we didn't have that far to go.

At 2:00 we stopped at Castlemaine, the hometown of the legendary Wild Colonial Boy. Actually we were just on the outskirts of the town. We parked and went looking for a pub where we could get a bite to eat. Across the little square where we had parked was a very tiny pub, the Castle Inn. We ordered a half-pint and asked if they served food. They didn't, so we contented ourselves with a couple of bags of peanuts.

We left the Castle Inn and headed for the car. Directly across the road was Griffin's, a rather plain little pub. We would have passed it up except that a high school classmate of mine, whom I run into frequently at Irish events and who lives across the street from Dan's parents, is named Jim Griffin. I thought he would be pretty put out if we passed up a pub with a name like that. So we went in and had a half-pint, just for sentimental purposes.

We left Castlemaine and followed R561 to Faranfore where we picked up N23 to Castleisland, and then N21 to Abbeyfeale, just inside County Limerick. We got to Abbeyfeale at 3:30, parked in the town centre, and walked around a bit. We made a stop into The Ploughman, mostly to use the toilet, but since the toilets are for customers' use only, well, you know the routine.

After our obligatory half-pint, we strolled around, just checking out Abbeyfeale, an unpretentious little rural market town of around 2000 people. We decided to have an early dinner this evening after we had checked into our B&B, so we noted a few landmarks for later use and headed out to our lodging for the night.

We had been given very easy directions to the place, about two miles out of town. It was a working farm/B&B called (Are you ready for this?) Fitzgerald's Farm. It seems that Fitzgeralds have pretty well sewed up the B&B business. Fitzgerald's consists of a big beautiful old house surrounded by horse pastures, the whole works overlooking the valley. The whole town is visible from the front yard, and at a distance is a perfect postcard view.

The lady of the house, Kathleen, showed us to our room, which has a nearly private entrance, access to a sun porch, and a little patio directly outside the door. We told Kathleen that we had tried to get a place in Listowel, about 10 miles away, but couldn't manage it. She said she wasn't surprised. This is the height of the racing season, and in this part of Ireland it can get to be a real passion. She told us we were lucky she had a vacancy when we called because all her rooms were now booked for tonight, most of the visitors people who had brought their horses to be boarded at the farm while the race meets were going on. She invited us to tour the grounds as much as we wished, and then left us to ourselves.

After we'd settled in, we poured ourselves a tad of Jameson's and went out to sit for awhile on the patio. In the rock wall that borders the patio, there is a profusion of flowers, surrounded by thousands of shamrocks. What a wonderful way to wind down today's journey.

After sitting for a bit, we took up on Kathleen's invitation to walk around the place. The Fitzgeralds have a sort of kids' petting zoo with all sorts of exotic birds, domestic ducks and geese, and of course, the inevitable sheep and goats, Since this is horse country, the farm also provides trail rides for guests who request it.

Before we left for town, Micki called Laurice to check on things in the US. We imagined that the whole country must surely be in chaos by now since we'd been gone nearly three weeks. We hadn't seen American television or read an American newspaper in all that time. Actually, it had been pretty nice. Laurice assured us that the country was creaking along without us and would probably survive until Sunday when we returned.

With that reassurance, we returned to Abbeyfeale for dinner. Kathleen had recommended a place called O'Riordan's and had said the food was good and reasonable. We found it, since we had noted it as a landmark a few hours earlier, and went in to have one at the bar. As we were sitting there, a big fellow sat down at the bar next to us. He bore a striking resemblance to Ronan Tynan, the Irish tenor: thin hair, round face, prominent ears (like mine) and an infectious grin.

Since pub manners prevail, we weren't surprised (or offended) when he struck up a conversation. After the usual "How are you enjoying your holiday?," we got to chatting about things in general. He was (and I hope still is) a police officer (*Gárda*) and had just gotten off duty and dropped into O'Riordan's to unwind. When Micki told him that she was a nurse in a small town hospital, the two of them had a grand old time comparing hairy emergency room stories. People who deal with the wreckage of humanity and the disasters that befall people have a sort of bond that defies all boundaries; they know and understand things that the rest of us are completely clueless about. It was an amazing and inspiring experience to listen to an American nurse and an Irish cop discuss the things they had in common.

Great as the conversation with the guard was, our table was waiting. He wished us a safe trip home and we went into the dining room. O'Riordan's is a sort of homey family place without a lot of classy surroundings. Still, we felt very comfortable and relaxed here. For dinner, Micki ordered the Chicken Kiev and I ordered the baked salmon. I knew that I was going to have salmon withdrawal symptoms when I got home; I'd eaten more salmon in the last three weeks than I had in the last five years. Anyway the meal didn't arrive at the table very fast, but we didn't care. We knew that our meals were being prepared from scratch and the quality would be worth it. Besides, we didn't have any deadlines to meet. We were starting to operate on Irish time.

After our dinner, we felt it necessary to visit one more pub before calling it a night. Right in front of where we had parked was O'Rourke's, an excellent place to stop in for an after dinner Paddy. This is a very old pub with a great deal of stonework and old wood. We parked ourselves by a fireplace and surveyed the place and its clientele. The place was fairly full, but pretty quiet and subdued. There were a lot of horsy types in there: riding breeches, tweed jackets and so on. Ireland may be a modern, democratic, classless republic, but traditions die hard and the old horse riding set will always be there.

When we left O'Rourke's to head home, all we had to do was head down the street and we'd be on the road to Fitzgerald's. However, we had to wait a while; there was a funeral home just a few doors down from O'Rourke's, and a wake was just being finished. A hearse pulled away from the funeral home and people were coming out and filling the street. It would be disrespectful to pull out in the middle of all this, and besides, you wouldn't be able to get through the crowd anyway. We watched the hearse proceed up the street. In the back where the casket was secured, the lights were on so one could see inside. The whole vehicle was stuffed with flowers, mostly wreaths with a ribbon inscribed "Uncle." Of course, we'll never know who "Uncle" was, but I sometimes wonder about him.

After the crowd in front of the funeral home dispersed, we started up the hill back to Fitzgerald's. The countryside in Ireland is usually very quiet and peaceful at night, and tonight was no exception. After a brief scan at the lights of Abbeyfeale, we retired.

DURTY NELLY'S SHIRT

SEPTEMBER 23. It was rainy and misty this morning, but it wasn't depressing; rather the rain made all that green just stand out even more. I went outside for a bit before breakfast to take a look at the valley. The clouds were low over the distant hills, covering the tops of some of the higher ones. The town of Abbeyfeale looked like a scene from some old romantic painting. I tried to soak in the scene as much as possible; it'll probably be a long time before I see it again. I also soaked up a lot of rain.

Breakfast was at 8:30 in a beautiful old dining room with a lot of antique furnishings. Micki loved that. Somehow, in Ireland antiques don't seem as much of a novelty as they are in the US. Many of the places we stayed at were furnished with antiques, but they seemed more like cherished family heirlooms than collectibles.

We were the first ones in the dining room but were soon joined by a couple of fellows, one a Californian and the other an Irishman. They were discussing horses so I figured they were here for the races at Listowel. The conversation soon drifted around to *Angela's Ashes.* Both these guys thought that the story was a gross exaggeration. The Irish guy was almost indignant that the movie especially was a great distortion. Well, I have no idea about that, but having seen Frank McCourt on stage in his one-man show *Irish Stew,* I wouldn't be surprised. Exaggeration for the sake of a good yarn has always been the staple of Irish storytellers.

We settled up with Kathleen and said our goodbyes. She suggested that as long as we were headed toward Limerick, we spend some time in the town of Adare which is right on the way. She said that people come from all over to visit and that it is a great attraction.

We left Abbeyfeale at 9:45 and headed up N21 toward Limerick. It was still a bit rainy, but it was starting to let up. There wasn't any visibility problem and the traffic was light. I guessed that this part of the country would be pretty well deserted, since the All-Ireland Football finals would be in Dublin on Sunday. This is like our Superbowl, and anybody who could get ahold of a ticket was going to be in Dublin.

We arrived in Adare at 10:30 and were certainly glad of Kathleen's suggestion. Adare is a very attractive town, whose main feature is the abundance of thatch-roofed buildings. Apparently, the citizens at some time decided that thatched houses were a good way to define the community. With the current tourist boom in Ireland, they've become quite an asset.

We found a parking spot on what looked like the main street and strolled around. Adare is pretty well oriented to the tourist trade. There are a lot of gift shops, art galleries and of course a block of all thatched houses, containing pricey merchandise like clothing and furniture.

The rain was little more than a mist now, but we left the cameras in the car to stay dry, and bought some postcards instead. By now, it was 11:00, and we certainly could not leave this picturesque town without a pub stop. Pat Collins' Bar was right across the street from where we had parked, so we went in for a half-pint. We savoured the Guinness slowly, knowing that after tomorrow, we'd be hard pressed to get the real thing.

Before leaving town, we stopped at the town Heritage Centre. Adare was an important stronghold for the powerful Fitzgerald dynasty during the Norman days, and the Heritage Centre has a large museum devoted to that era. There were quite a few tour buses unloading at the time, and the museum charged an admission fee, so we skipped it and just browsed through the free areas. I bought a couple of books to read on the plane, and we left.

Our destination for the evening was Bunratty, just a few miles from the airport. We figured that the closer we would be on the last night, the fewer hassles getting to the airport. Adare is only about ten miles from Limerick and Bunratty is just a few miles east of the city.

There is a very good bypass around Limerick, and we negotiated the city without any difficulty, and turned onto N18. At this point, the high-way widens into a dual carriageway as it heads toward the airport. Within a few minutes, we were in Bunratty. Our B&B, Bunratty Villa, is about a half-mile away from Bunratty Castle. We went directly there and checked in, unloaded a few things, and headed back to the castle.

The castle is not the only attraction at Bunratty. There is also the world famous Durty Nelly's Pub. No trip to Ireland would be complete (for anybody) without a visit to this prestigious watering hole. We had a few extra reasons to visit. Ronan Tynan, the famed Irish tenor, sang here occasionally during his student days; Santina and Dan had visited here on their honeymoon and insisted that we not return home without having been there; and finally, we had visited, on several occasions, a bar in Deadwood SD named Durty Nelly's. We thought it obligatory to visit the original. In fact, we had brought along a tee shirt from the Deadwood bar to present to someone at the Bunratty pub if the occasion arose.

Durty Nelly's is another place that's been in continuous operation for a few centuries. It's just across the street from Bunratty Castle, and apparently was an inn and stagecoach stop in its earlier days. Now it's an extremely popular tourist attraction.

It was 1:00 when we parked behind the building and walked around to the front door. There were several tour buses parked in front, and lunch was in full swing. The interior of the pub doesn't look like it has been changed for at least two hundred years. The door is small, the ceilings are low, and there are little passageways running to who knows where all over the place.

When we entered, we were greeted by the sound of a bunch of American drunks slurring out "When Irish Eyes Are Smiling" at the top of their very untuneful voices somewhere in a back room. I had hoped that I wouldn't hear that in Ireland, and I almost succeeded. I fell into it on our last day in Ireland.

The little pub area was extremely crowded, but we managed to grab a small table when another couple left. It was at this point that I encountered for the first and only time on our trip, anything like rude behaviour on the part of an Irish server; and it was my own fault. The place was packed, the bar was full, and the serving staff were doing their best to keep up. I went up to the bar, waited a few moments until I got a waitress's attention, and asked if I could have a couple of menus. She snapped at me, "Could you wait just a minute, please?" then finished what she was doing and handed me the menus. I thanked her as apologetically as I could and went back to the table rather embarrassed.

By now the lunch crowd was thinning out. The tour buses started loading their passengers for a mad dash to the next stop. Apparently tour bus vacationers have short attention spans, as they never seem to stay in one spot for long.

A waitress came over to the table and we ordered our lunch. Frommer had recommended avoiding the higher priced dining room at Durty Nelly's and eating the better tasting and cheaper pub food. He was right again. I had fish and chips, and Micki had the roast beef special of the day. Very plentiful, very tasty, and very satisfying, but we'd come to expect that.

It was still raining outside, so we just sat for a while, sipping our pints and enjoying the atmosphere. When the waitress came to clear our table, it was the same girl who had snapped at me about the menus. Since it was now a lot quieter and calmer, I apologized and said that I didn't mean to be pushy before. She smiled and said that that was all right, things were a little tense then and she hadn't meant to be rude. Now that we were buddies again, I took out the tee shirt with Durty Nelly's-Deadwood on it, and presented it to her. She was thrilled, thanked me profusely, and scampered back behind the bar. When we got up to leave, I could see her in a back room showing off the shirt to some of the other girls. They seemed to be impressed.

Across the road from Durty Nelly's is a complex of buildings, a combination of very new and modern, and a few old ones that were probably part of the original village. This has all been turned into a shopping and entertainment complex called the Bunratty Village Mill. We wandered around here for awhile, and then crossed a little park to the Creamery Pub. I guess this really was a creamery at one time, as there are old cream cans and various types of machinery around the place as decor. It was a pretty big place, but enjoyable, as it was simply a pub without a lot of touristy things. They also serve meals, so we checked out their menu for dinner possibilities.

We went back across the road to take a peek at Bunratty Castle and Folk Park. The castle is right on the road and the folk park is on the grounds behind it. An admission ticket gets you into both places.

We went more or less directly to Bunratty Castle itself. I don't know how much restoration work has been done on it, but it's quite impressive. Visitors are given a map/floor plan of the place and encouraged to wander around at their own pace. There are several large halls inside decorated with what looks like the original furnishings. The Great Hall is the site of the nightly Medieval Banquet that is staged for visitors. We had decided earlier to skip that, but we enjoyed our self-tour around the place.

The castle is all of six stories high, with each floor connected to the next by a tiny spiral stone staircase at each corner. People in the Middle Ages must have been considerably smaller than modern people, as the staircases were barely big enough for one person to navigate. Occasionally on the way up, we would discover a small room off the stairs that was furnished as a bedroom or sitting room. It was at these places that the tourist traffic got straightened out. If we'd see someone coming from the opposite direction, we'd just squeeze into the small room and let them go by. Others did the same for us.

Eventually we made it to the top of the castle and looked out over the parapet onto the River Shannon. The land around this part of the Shannon is mostly low bog, not much good for anything, except that it's flat enough, and was probably cheap enough, to build a big international airport, and that's just what they did. It's a little mind bending to stand on the top of a fourteenth century castle and watch 747's float down to a runway five miles away.

After leaving the castle we directed our attention to the rest of the grounds. With a name like Bunratty Folk Park, you might imagine some sort of Disneyesque phoney recreation of a cute Irish village of days of yore with quaint little people running around saying "Shure and begorrah!" for the amusement of tourists. It wasn't like that at all. It was more like a museum. The Folk Park was designed by Kevin Danaher, a respected Irish historian and folklorist whose concept was to present to visitors an authentic depiction of Irish rural life in times past. Actual buildings had been moved intact from all parts of Ireland and arranged in the same way they might have been in a real village.

The idea of the village is to show and preserve the various types of rural architecture, with examples of each showing how various classes of people carried out their daily lives. Each house was furnished in accordance with its probable inhabitants, from the poorest day labourer's cottage to the relatively wealthy farmer's house. In addition, a small business district had been relocated on the grounds to complete the impression of a whole village.

There were plenty of museum pieces on the premises, but they weren't isolated in glass cases with little explanatory tags attached. They were all placed in the various houses where they would most likely have been put when they were in use.

One house we visited had an ongoing demonstration of bread making as it was done in times past. The lady doing the demonstration was a hearty cheery type who said that she had made bread like this when she was a girl. She explained that most of rural Ireland didn't get electricity until the 1960's, so there were a lot of people around that remember how things were done in the "old days." She also told us that the house we were in had been moved to the park when Shannon Airport was built in the late 1950's. In fact, it had sat right where the main runway is now located.

We went up a slight incline to the "downtown" part of the village. All the buildings had been moved in from someplace else, but they were arranged very naturally and it appeared that they had always been there. Some of the stores were gift shops actually operating and others were simply there as examples. Of course, the most active place on the town square was Mac's Pub. Naturally we couldn't resist.

Mac's has several little bar and dining areas, probably the most interesting being the kitchen bar, where guests sit around an old kitchen table right next to a working fireplace. We sipped our half-pints and watched the clientele for a while, and then finished touring the park.

We made one more stop, Kathleen's Pub in the Bunratty Hotel. This is on the other side of the road from the castle. We recrossed the road yet again and went into Kathleen's for just one more.

The whole place is fairly new, but the pub is designed and decorated to look like it's pretty old. It's a fairly comfortable place. When we took our places at the bar and ordered, there was another couple already seated, with one empty stool between them and Micki. Out of nowhere, a cute little blond girl about three years old climbed up on the empty barstool and placed her empty bottle on the bar. Even though nobody understood her, she babbled away as if we all did. Micki thought she understood her to say her name was Teresa. Apparently, she wanted her bottle refilled. Without batting an eye, the young barman took the bottle, filled it with milk, warmed it in a little steamer, and handed it back to Teresa as if he does this all the time.

Her mother appeared just now and was pretty relieved to find her. She had wandered off from some other part of the building, and the whole family was about to go into a panic. Teresa didn't seem to be very upset at all. Later Micki encountered her again in the ladies room, this time with her mother. She found out that Teresa's name was really Shauna, and, according to her mother, "was really something." No exaggeration there.

We left Kathleen's and made our way back to Bunratty Villa to tidy up a bit and get as much stuff together as possible to avoid having to pack tomorrow. I called Aer Lingus at Shannon to confirm our flight and was assured that it was on schedule.

We decided to have our last dinner in Ireland at the Creamery, and to make it as traditional as possible, so we both ordered the Irish stew. It was delicious, full of big tasty chunks of lamb, potatoes, carrots, and onions. We hadn't been much on desserts, mostly because the meals were so generous we didn't have any room, but tonight we decided to go for it. Micki had the warm apple pie with fresh whipped cream. Piecrust in Ireland is more soft and cake-like than crusts on pie in the US, exceptionally tasty though. I had the most outrageous concoction called chocolate lumpy-bumpy. It was a sort of ice cream dish filled with chunks of chocolate, marshmallows, and nuts. The whole works was then drenched in chocolate sauce and whipped cream. Definitely the most decadent thing I've ever eaten.

We left the Creamery and returned to the car out in the parking lot. It was dark by now, and just as I was about to put the key in the ignition, the lens fell out of my glasses again. I retrieved the lens, but lost the screw that is supposed to hold the frame together. We still had the repair kit that we had bought in Dublin, but trying to do a repair in the dark would be impossible. We went back into the Creamery, explained our predicament, and the barmaid very graciously let us use a well lit table to make the repair. Fortunately, there was a spare screw in the kit, and Micki made the repair in short order. I couldn't see anything that small.

The rest of the evening was uneventful. We made a second stop at Mac's, hoping for a little traditional music, but they weren't going to start until late, so we sipped a whiskey and returned to Bunratty Villa for our last night in Ireland.

SLÁN ABHAILE

**SEPTEMBER 24.** Well, today was the day we return to reality. It was all over but the plane ride home. We went into the dining room to enjoy our last breakfast in Ireland. We both opted for the traditional Irish breakfast as a sort of farewell. Our host Jack, a very friendly fellow, served it to us. It was delicious. The only thing that marred breakfast was the obnoxious behaviour of our fellow guests; all Americans headed for Chicago today, unfortunately on our flight. Micki said she was grateful for very large airliners. We bid Jack goodbye and apologized for the behaviour of our fellow Americans, assuring him that most of us know how to behave.

We got out to Shannon at 10:00, after a very short drive. We turned into the airport on the same roundabout we had left on nearly three weeks ago, but by this time we had gotten a grasp of driving in Ireland, and we took it pretty much for granted.

There was very little traffic around the airport, and we went directly to the Avis lot to return Clio. I noticed that the cover of the rear-view mirror on the driver's side was missing, but I didn't have a clue as to where it had gone.

We unloaded our luggage and went into the office to return the keys. I told the lady behind the counter about the missing mirror cover. She looked into the paperwork and informed me that it had been missing when we picked up the car. She went out to check the car for damage, gave it a cursory once over, and came back in to tell me that everything was fine.

We were shuttled back to the terminal in the Avis courtesy mini-bus. Along with us was a couple from North Dakota. We chatted with them and the driver on the way to the terminal. We Americans were surprised that there was so little traffic around the terminal, and the driver informed us that Shannon was a pretty casual place, no stress or hassles.

There were very few people in the terminal building, and we had no trouble checking in and getting our boarding passes, both for the Aer Lingus flight to Chicago and our connecting flight on American Airlines to Minneapolis.

The duty free shop in the departure area wasn't open yet so we had a cup of coffee in a cafeteria and filled out some immigration papers that were necessary for departing Ireland. When the duty free shop opened at 11:00, we made our way into the departure area. Once through the gate, we were technically out of the country. Anything purchased duty free could not be taken into Ireland, since Irish taxes had not been applied.

The departure area and the duty free shop are very modern and spacious. There is plenty of comfortable seating for waiting, and the shopping area is almost like a mall. We browsed through the shops for awhile and Micki bought a few last-minute souvenirs.

I had been told before the trip that there is an excellent scotch unavailable in the US: Johnny Walker Green Label, a fifteen-year-old single malt. I looked around the fairly extensive liquor shop, but didn't see it. I finally asked a clerk if they carried it. He directed me to a corner shelf and there it was—one bottle. I made a mad dash to grab that last bottle and got it before anyone else did. I've told people since that I trampled a nun getting that little treasure, but I didn't really. I just kicked her out of the way.

Being in Ireland, naturally there is a bar available for travellers who wish to savour the refreshments of Ireland for the last time. Micki was still browsing around the shops, so I sat at the bar and had a final pint of genuine Guinness. I got to talking with an American lady who was on her way home today too. She had been to many of the places we had visited, so we compared notes. She was nice enough, but she seemed to think the Irish were slightly dim-witted. I don't know where she got that impression; I thought most of the dimwits I saw were Americans.

When Micki finished her shopping and we had changed our money back to US dollars, we felt that it was necessary to a have a couple of Irish coffees. The classic Irish coffee was invented right here where we were sitting. When Shannon International opened in the late fifties, Joe Sheridan the bartender in this very bar came up with this delectable concoction of Irish whiskey, coffee and whipped cream. In fact, there is a large plaque on the wall, commemorating Joe and Irish coffee.

The shops and the bar in the departure area take any currency, so we purchased our coffees in dollars, the first time in nearly three weeks that we had American money in our pockets.

Our flight was scheduled to leave at 1:00 and boarding was to begin at 12:20. We went through immigration without difficulty, but had a long wait of nearly an hour before we boarded the plane. It turned out that our flight was not going directly to O'Hare from Shannon, but was making a brief stop in Dublin. The boarding delay was in getting the domestic passengers bound for Dublin on the plane first, where they were seated in the front of the plane, so they could get off quickly.

We were finally aboard and took off a little over an hour behind schedule. Since it's only about 150 miles from Shannon to Dublin, the plane never gained much altitude. We were fortunate to have a window seat so we could get a good look at the countryside on the short 30-minute flight to Dublin.

The stop in Dublin was very brief and we were soon on our way. The captain came on the loudspeaker and apologized for the delay but assured everyone that we would make any connecting flights without any difficulty. He also told us that he'd be keeping tabs on the All-Ireland Finals and would inform us of anything significant.

So what's to tell about an international airplane flight? It was smooth and comfortable and long. I let my mind drift back over the last three weeks and tried to pick out an experience I would have changed. There was none. I had walked where Collins, Pearse and De Valera had walked. I had seen the resting-places of Swift and Strongbow. I had visited the hangouts of Behan and Joyce. Most importantly, I had rubbed shoulders with hundreds of ordinary Irish people and had come to appreciate their cheeriness, their impeccable manners, their wit and imagination, and above all, their love of poetry, music and song. No, there was nothing I would have changed.

We were taking a northern route and the captain came on the horn at one point to inform us that we were flying over Iceland, and at another time that we were flying over Greenland. We could see the mountains and glaciers of Greenland as we flew over. I thought that according to Sean back in Doolin, who said he had visited Minnesota by flying over it, we could now say we had been to Iceland and Greenland.

Somewhere over Northern Canada, the captain announced that the All Ireland Finals between Galway and Kerry had ended in a tie. I didn't quite understand that. I guess Gaelic football doesn't provide for sudden death overtime.

We arrived at O'Hare at about 5:30 and made a mad dash for the baggage carousel. We'd been assured that we could catch our connection to Minneapolis, but the time was getting a little short. The attendants from our flight on Aer Lingus were right at the carousel assisting people with their luggage. I'd never seen that before. We got our bags and were waved through customs without a glance. I suspect our smooth talking flight attendants had something to do with that. I also suspect the Irish influence in Chicago might have been at work too.

Immediately after customs, our bags were automatically rechecked through to Minneapolis. We ran for the shuttle to take us to the domestic terminal, but this time with much more confidence, as we were a little more familiar with the system.

We arrived at the American Airlines gate just as passengers were beginning to board. We presented our boarding passes and were told that one of our seats was already occupied. The lady stamping boarding passes was very nice and said that the mistake had been made in Shannon and she'd try to get it straightened out. However, the young smart aleck behind the desk kept yelling at the passengers to hurry up and get aboard. There were a number of people on standby and several volunteering to be bumped. All the while we were standing there, this guy kept hollering that the plane was about to leave.

After fifteen minutes of this nonsense, I blew up. I told the young wise guy in mildly profane language to get his act together and get us aboard NOW. He grumbled a little but lost a good deal of his arrogance and said he was only trying to get us seats together. He got us aboard in very short order with the explanation that we now had better seats than before. I didn't get that since the aircraft was a very small commuter jet and there weren't any particularly good seats.

Once aboard and in the air, my wrath at American Airlines was dissipated by one of the flight attendants. This was a very pleasant African-American lady with a great sense of humour. As she was beginning to bring the beverage cart down the very narrow centre aisle, she yelled out to the passengers, "Better get your arms and legs out of the aisle now! You're going to need those body parts when we land!"

The flight to Minneapolis was only fifty minutes and we were on the ground at 8:10 Central Time. We got our baggage in good order and Laurice picked us up and brought us to their home in St. Louis Park.

We were far too disoriented from flying, time changes, baggage chasing and putting arrogant little pups in their place to drive home to Melrose that night. Instead we regaled the Magills with our adventures. We probably didn't make much sense. At one point we mentioned that we had bought a cool CD in Wales that had "Give Me That Old Time Religion" sung entirely in Welsh. Steve deadpanned, "Oh, Gee! I certainly wouldn't have come home without one of those."

We were home, and it was good to be back, but there will always be times when I mentally revisit Doolin, Carrick, Ardmayle, and Dingle. I like to imagine that those beautiful places will always welcome us back and be home to us too.

UGLY AMERICANS

I debated with myself quite a bit about including the following material. I didn't want to promote stereotypes or to appear as a carping, complaining snob. I realize that well-mannered people of whatever nationality are invisible, but boorishness stands out like a sore thumb. Of course, there are differences between Irish and American codes of etiquette, and I am sure that we inadvertently broke a few rules. However, we found it disturbing to see so many fellow Americans behaving quite badly in Ireland. They seemed to relish reinforcing the stereotypical image of the crude Yankee that so many countries have of us. Our own personal attitude is that visitors in other countries are guests and should behave accordingly.

The Irish people seemed to us to be generous, cheerful and hospitable people. They enjoy the company of others and will go out of their way to make travelers comfortable. Yet we saw so many American tourists treat their hosts as inferiors and their hosts' manners and customs with ill-concealed condescending contempt.

Food seems to be a focal point of bad manners. Americans, and especially Midwesterners (at least in my estimation), tend to view anything that varies from the customary as ostentatious. Anything "different" is viewed with suspicion. I first noticed this mind-set during our first breakfast at Churchfield B&B in Doolin. Admittedly, the Full Irish Breakfast is very different from an American breakfast, but we considered the heartiness and variety of the meal to be an intriguing adventure. There were a number of other Americans at breakfast with us, and I was dismayed at the comments I heard: "What the hell's this?" "Yuk!" "Don't they have any real food?" I surmised that a bowl of soggy Cheerios would have sent them into ecstasy.

We noticed after a very short time in Ireland that the Irish are generally a soft-spoken people. We seldom heard a voice raised above a conversational level, with the understandable exception of the excitement of a sporting event. Americans, however, unfortunately can be loud to the point of embarrassment. When we were spending our second day in Dublin and I was sitting at the bar in the Lord Kildare on Nassau Street waiting for Micki to finish her yarn shopping, four American women came in for a drink. I had sat at the bar for ten minutes waiting for someone to show up to serve me. The lunch crowd had just left and the servers were busy cleaning up. I was served when someone was available and I thought little of it.

However, these four women were scarcely seated when they began yelling "Hey! Is anybody there? Excuse me! Can we get some service?" The other patrons in the place looked extremely embarrassed. A barman, attracted by the racket, came and took their orders and they momentarily quieted down.

I was as embarrassed as anyone else in the place, and in a perhaps futile attempt to clue them in, started up a conversation with them. They were from Wisconsin, and when I told them I was from Minnesota, they considered me as some sort of neighbor and started to tell me about their experiences so far in Ireland. They had temporarily escaped their tour bus and were seeking relief from their tour guides who had apparently admonished them about their obnoxious behavior on the bus. Other passengers had complained that their loud laughter and screeching was becoming annoying. Far from being contrite, they were offended that anyone would complain about their "just having fun." They were completely oblivious to the sensibilities of others.

I suspect that part of the problem is unrealistic expectations. I'm afraid that many American tourists don't realize that in other countries there are real people living their ordinary lives the way they always did, and have developed a system of living that works for them. That system may not be familiar to average Americans who unfortunately have a great deal of arrogance about their own way of life and tend to look down on anything that differs from the American way.

At least part of the fault can be placed on the travel industry. In an effort to promote tourism, exaggerated images are floated before prospective tourists—thatched houses, jaunting carts, wizened little men sitting on rock walls with a pipe and a witty comment for the passing traveler. The reality is, at least in Ireland today, that cell phones, computers, television, and upscale fashions are nearly as commonplace as in the US.

Another part of the problem is just plain ignorance. Americans are notoriously clueless about the folkways and habits of other countries. The result is that guided tours are popular. People take bus tours for the convenience, of course, but also with the attitude that they're being conducted through some sort of open-air zoo, much like Busch Gardens.

An example of this surfaced in Fishguard, Wales. While we were waiting for our lunch to be prepared in the Royal Oak Inn, two obviously American couples entered. They attracted attention immediately because of their dress. One of the women in particular stood out. She had long stringy bleached blond hair, was wearing obscenely tight leggings, a leopard-skin print top with a feather boa, and colored foil stars pasted on her face. The whole ensemble was topped with a yachting cap.

The women sat down at a table and the men went up to the bar to order their lunch. Since we were in Wales and leeks are a part of the cuisine (at least for tourists), the chalkboard menus all over the place featured a wide variety of leek dishes. Completely oblivious to the menus, one of the men asked the young girl behind the bar if they served leeks. I watched with growing amusement as a curtain of "dumb foreigner stupidity" dropped down her face. She looked him right in the eye and without a blink declared in that long-vowelled Welsh accent: "Noooo."

He took her word for it, placed an order for something else, and returned to his table. It wasn't three minutes before one of the women went up to the bar to see if their lunches were ready. One of the group would repeat this about every five minutes after that, with the explanation that the bus was leaving soon. We watched this spectacle as we leisurely dined on our leek curries. The lunches finally arrived and our compatriots bolted them, settled up and dashed out the door, presumably to get on the bus and rush to another place where they could act equally stupid. The waitress cleaned their table with a noticeable attitude of relief. I left her a big tip.

It seemed that our encounters with rude Americans always occurred when we were eating. At our supper at Oliver St. John Gogarty's in Dublin, we were treated to the spectacle of eight Americans having dinner at a nearby table. They drew attention to themselves not only by their loud voices and braying laughter, but also by the way the treated their waitress. They thought it was quite amusing to change their drink orders several times, and then make loud disparaging remarks about Irish food. Burger King, a few blocks away on Graffton Street, would have probably been more satisfying to them. Better yet, they should have stayed home.

I mentioned previously the prattling fool in Davern's in Cashel. I won't give him any attention here because it's a safe bet that he was a jerk in the US too. Anybody that obnoxious probably is that way anywhere he goes.

Probably the most annoying bunch of Ugly Americans was the crew that stayed at Bunratty Villa with us on our final night in Ireland. Jack Burns, the owner of the place, is an extremely decent and gracious host. His dining room is attractive and airy, and equipped with beautiful furniture.

This bunch of morons amused themselves by asking Jack inane questions, prefacing each one with "Oh, Jack!" When Jack would answer their foolishness, they would laugh and imitate his accent. They also got their kicks by asking for things that were not on the breakfast menu and were obviously not available. When we had finished our delicious breakfast and were leaving the dining room, I noticed that one of the guys in the group had his muddy feet up on the beautiful hand embroidered seat of one of the chairs.

When we left Bunratty Villa, I apologized to Jack for the crude behavior of our fellow Americans. Jack, being the gentleman that he is, just shrugged and remarked that they weren't as bad as some that he'd seen.

If there was anything disappointing about our three weeks in Ireland, it was the behavior of too many American tourists.

SOME RECOMMENDATIONS

Although I've stated at the beginning that this is not a travel book, for anyone contemplating a trip to Ireland, I do have a few recommendations based solely on my own experience and what worked well for us. I don't care for surprises, particularly nasty ones, so good planning is the key to a successful trip. Laying groundwork is very important, so that the visitor has some idea what to expect.

As a preliminary step in planning a vacation to Ireland, I would strongly recommend purchasing a good detailed travel guide. We used Frommer's *Ireland from $50 a Day* and found it invaluable. This book is reissued regularly with updated information. Very likely the current edition is up to $65 to $70 a day by now. The book is full of details on history, climate, accomodations, and maps. We took our copy with us and used it as a resource every day.

Once you have a general idea of your itinerary, contact the Irish Tourist Board (*Bord Failte*) at 800-223-6470 or the Northern Ireland Tourist Board at 800-326-0036. Ask for information on attractions and accommodations, and they will send you all the material you would want. *Bord Failte* also has an excellent website: ***www.ireland.travel.ie***. The Northern Ireland Tourist Board also has an informative website: ***www.interknowledge.com/northern-ireland***. There is an amazing amount of information available on bothe sites, including all the listings in the Gulliver system of booking reservations. I strongly encourage visiting these websites for the latest information.

My recommendation for economical lodging is bed and breakfasts. We didn't experience a bad one on the entire trip. If you are interested in this type of accommodation, ask the Tourist Board for a listing of approved bed and breakfasts. For even more detailed information, visit the accommodations pages on the Tourist Board website.

If you decide to rent a car, and I strongly recommend it, obtain the Collins *Road Atlas Ireland*. I believe it is the most complete and detailed piece of information a driver could have. It depicts all roads in Ireland, including the North, in large-scale format. We found it invaluable. If the atlas cannot be found at local bookstores, try the Harper-Collins website ***www.fireandwater.com.***

I would consider three items of information essential on a driving tour of Ireland: Frommer's guide, the Town&Country Homes Association list of B&B's, and Collins road atlas. Any other information can be obtained as you go.

Frommer's guide also contains an excellent capsule history of Ireland and a good number of sidebars on Irish culture. A broad and entertaining view of Ireland and the Irish can be obtained from the many CD's and videos available. They can give a prospective visitor a wide look at all things Irish, and from many viewpoints.

To get a grasp of Irish traditional music, I'd suggest the many Chieftains' albums. This group has popularized the traditional music of the Irish countryside, and has succeeded in keeping it authentic. The Chieftains have managed to preserve the sound that you hear in any spontaneous pub session in the country.

For a good sample of Irish ballads, I would recommend the reissued albums of the Clancy Brothers and Tommy Makem. Bobby Clancy, Liam Clancy, Tommy Makem and their families are still producing records, and I'd suggest checking them out.

The Irish movie industry has come to the forefront in the last decade and has produced some excellent films on Irish life. Of course, there are still the old classic films available on video, in particular the ever popular *The Quiet Man*. This movie is chockfull of stereotypes and cliches, but is done with such good humor and tongue-in-cheek exaggeration that it's still enjoyable after fifty years. The brooding and disquieting *Ryan's Daughter* gives a dark view of the Irish struggle for independance.

More recent films portray various aspects of Ireland. *The Secret of Roan Inish* and *The Seventh Stream* are modern retellings of the old Celtic myth of the selkie, the mysterious seal-people. *Cal* portrays the personal tragedies spawned by the Troubles in Ulster. *The Crying Game, The Name of the Father,* and *The Boxer* deal with the same theme. Neil Jordan's excellent *Michael Collins* offers a tentative explanation of Collins' death. The film adaptation of Brian Friel's play *Dancing at Lunasa* and *This is my Father* both examine the devastating effect of poverty and class distinctions in Ireland in the early twentieth century. *Waking Ned Devine* and *the Matchmaker* are excellent examples of hilarious Irish tall tales. *Ned Devine* features the most unique motorcycle ride on film, and *The Matchmaker* offers an uproarious sendup of Americans searching for their Irish roots.

These resources are simply a good place to start. More detailed information can be found as plans become more focused. In addition, the Tourist Board has information centers in nearly every town. City maps, lists of local attractions and accommodations are readily available at these places. We found information centers staffed by congenial young people who were always courteous and helpful.

There is one final item that bears mentioning—driving on the left. Driving habits and the rules of the road are fairly ingrained in every driver. To drive in a country where everything you've learned is turned around can be very disconcerting. However, the change from right to left is not as difficult as it would seem. Of course, American drivers need to concentrate more and keep a higher state of alertness than they ordinarily would, but road markings are fairly clear. Visibility, speed, and narrow country roads pose a far greater threat than left-hand traffic. A good rule of thumb to follow is to drive only fast enough so that you can stop within your present range of vision. Twisting regional roads with no margin of safety on the edges can be potential disasters.

Irish drivers aren't particularly speed-crazy, and we found them to be generally courteous. Upon spotting an approaching car, it's a good idea to slow down to a crawl, move as far to the left as possible, and let the other car pass by. It's also courteous to pull into a driveway and let a following car go ahead. It's also a way of getting rid of a distraction.

AFTERWORD

Since our sojourn in Ireland, the world has changed dramatically. The American economy has crashed into a recession, and I assume the effects have been felt on the Irish economy. What was once extolled in the late 1990's as the "Celtic Tiger," the bright star of the new Europe, has probably been somewhat dimmed. The peaks and valleys of any economy are a reality of history. Still, just as the American economy will recover, so will Ireland's.

The horrible effects of the terrorist attacks in the US on September 11, 2001, were felt worldwide. I surmise that the fear of flying that presently prevails cut deeply into the Irish economy, which relies heavily on tourism. I don't believe that it will last for long. The things that attracted visitors to Ireland—the magnificent scenery, the music and dance, and above all the generous hospitality of the Irish people—are still intact. When the world rebounds, these things will be ready and waiting.

Beginning in January 2002, Irish currency will be replaced by the euro. The various denominations of Irish pounds will cease to exist as of July 2002. I realize that the change is probably a smart economic move, but I find the change to be rather sad. I liked the various bills with their dramatic portrayal of Ireland's heroes and the official print in Gaelic. Heroic portraits of Eamon DeValera, Daniel O'Connell and the rest will be replaced on paper currency with cold modern designs that depict a generic symbol of the future—efficient but without a soul.

However, I'm confident that the really important things will not change in Ireland. The manners, the wit, the generosity of the

Irish people are unchanging. And after all, isn't that the heart of a nation?

CONCLUSIONS

So what did we learn in three weeks of traveling all over Ireland? I personally learned that my preconceived notions about the country were not wrong, but they were incomplete. I knew that the Irish were a charming and gracious people, and I discovered that it was true and more. I suspected but did not know the full extent of thousands of years of history around you at all times. I realized that as a people, we Americans are young and raw and have much to learn.

I learned that time and distance are not the same in all places. Americans consider Plymouth Rock to be an old historic site, but contemplating Newgrange makes that notion naive. I learned that doing things on schedule is less important than doing them well. What appears to be a lackadaisical attitude in Ireland is really a slow careful approach to life.

I learned that much of the bombastic rhetoric about Northern Ireland by Irish-Americans is mainly empty noise from a safe distance. It's easy to spout nationalistic slogans in Chicago or Boston; the reality is far more complex. I found Ulster to be a beautiful province nearly identical in appearance to Wisconsin. I was never aware of meeting a Protestant or Catholic in Ulster, only ordinary people whose daily lives are much like our own. Yet the Troubles are real—alleys strung with razor wire and armed troops supervising cash transfers at a bank. I think that the hope is very gradually becoming the reality: that the ridiculous posturing of thugs on both sides will be recognized for what it is—a wasteful throwback to times that are past and long gone.

Ireland is no longer a poverty stricken land of losers. The booming economy of the late nineties has made it one of the most prosperous countries in Europe. However, it seems that many Americans would rather see the Irish as poor, humble, and quaint. Their disappointment is obvious and irritating to the Irish. We were told on several occasions that we didn't act like Americans, and we took that as a compliment.

My wish for the future is that the Irish can keep accommodating the past, present, and future the way they now seem to be doing. May they never forget Cromwell's atrocities, but remember they happened 350 years ago. May they keep improving the roads, but never stop walking their dogs on quiet evenings. May they never become too self-important to pause and pass the time of day with a stranger. May they never lose their love of music and poetry and their love of the beauty of words. Above all, may the Irish never stop being the kind, humorous hospitable people we found them all to be.

ABOUT THE AUTHOR

Jesse Lovelace is a former English and Latin teacher. He has been a photographer, sales representative, and factory worker. He has an interest in all things Celtic: music, history, literature and language. He is currently a substitute teacher in Melrose, Minnesota.

0-595-23931-5

MILITARY MACHINES

[TANKS!]

QEB Publishing

Picture Credits:
Alamy 18-19 Colin C. Hill
Corbis 4-5 John A. Giordano, 6-7 Shane A. Cuomo,
20-21 Mike Buytas/U.S. Air Force /CNP 22-23 © CORBIS
defenceimages.mod.uk 2 WO2 Pete Bristo MBE
Getty FC Stocktrek Images, 10-11 David Higgs, 12-13 Stocktrek Images,

Editor: Lauren Taylor
Designer: Izzy Langridge
Educational consultant: Jillian Harker

Copyright © QEB Publishing, Inc. 2012

First published in the United States
by QEB Publishing, Inc
3 Wrigley Suite A
Irvine, CA 92618

www.qed-publishing.co.uk

ISBN 978 1 60992 290 0

Printed in China

A CIP record for this title is available from the Library of Congress.

Words in **bold** appear in
the glossary on page 24

CONTENTS

What Is a Tank?

A tank is a sort of fighting vehicle. It has a big gun on top and thick metal plates called **armor** to keep it safe. Tanks are big, heavy vehicles that move along on strong metal **tracks**.

In a battle, tanks attack enemy tanks and other vehicles. They also help, or support, soldiers who fight on foot.

Hull and Turret

The bottom part of a tank is called the **hull**. The top is called the **turret**. The turret can spin around so the crew can point the gun where they want.

The hull and turret are covered with armor. There are small doors called **hatches** in the turret.

turret

hull

Tank Tracks

Tank tracks are made of lots of metal pieces joined together with hinges, so they can bend. The tracks stop the tank from sinking into soft mud. They also grip well so the tank can climb steep hills.

The driver can make the tank spin around by making one track go forward and the other go backward.

The Tank Crew

A crew is a group of soldiers who work the tank. The crew of a main battle tank is made up of a commander, a driver, a gunner, and a loader. The commander is in charge.

The driver sits in the hull, using levers to drive the tank. The others sit in the turret. They see what is happening outside through a **periscope**.

periscope

Weapons

The main weapon on a tank is its big gun. The gun fires large shells that explode when they hit their target.

A computer aims and fires the gun.
It is very exact, and can hit a target
more than a mile away. A tank also has
machine guns in the turret and hull.

Main Battle Tanks

The biggest and heaviest tanks are called main battle tanks. A main battle tank weighs more than 55 tons (50 tonnes). That is as much as 50 family cars. The armor is made of metal and very strong plastic.

On some parts of the turret, it is more than 3 feet (1 meter) thick. Main battle tanks fight in bunches. They attack together and defend each other.

M1 Abrams

The M1 Abrams is the main battle tank of the United States **Army**. It has a 120-millimeter gun, which means the shells it fires are 120 millimeters across.

FACTS

Length	32.1 feet (9.8 meters)
Width	12.1 feet (3.7 meters)
Height	7.8 feet (2.4 meters)
Weight	69.4 tons (63 tonnes)
Top speed	41.6mph (67 kph)
Main gun	120-millimeter gun
Machine guns	3
Crew	4 people

Challenger 2

The Challenger 2 is the main
battle tank of the British Army.
It can fight in any weather,
in the daytime, and
even at night.

FACTS

Length	38 feet (11.6 meters)
Width	11.4 feet (3.5 meters)
Height	8.2 feet (2.5 meters)
Weight	68.8 tons (62.5 tonnes)
Top speed	36.6 mph (59 kph)
Main gun	120-millimeter gun
Machine guns	2
Crew	4 people

Infantry Fighting Vehicles

An **infantry** fighting vehicle is like a small tank. It can carry soldiers around the battlefield quickly. It has a lot of space inside for soldiers and equipment.

On top of the vehicle is a small turret and a small gun. Infantry fighting vehicles help soldiers in battle by firing at enemy soldiers.

Early Tanks

Tanks were invented about 100 years ago. Armies first used them during World War I, which lasted from 1914 to 1918.

The first tank to go into battle was a British tank called the Mark 1. It was very slow and often broke down. It also got stuck in deep mud on the battlefield, but it did help win some battles.

GLOSSARY

armor
A metal covering to protect against harm

army
A large number of people ready and trained for warfare

hatch
A door that covers an opening in a tank

hull
The armored body of a tank

infantry
Soldiers trained to fight on foot

periscope
A sort of tube that lets the user see above eye-level

tracks
Metal bands that tanks have instead of tires

turret
A small tower-like part on a tank that has a gun fixed to it